Pedigree Cats & Kittens
How to choose and care for them

Pedigree Cats & Kittens

How to choose and care for them

Paddy Cutts and Christina Payne

ARCO PUBLISHING, INC. New York

Great Britain and North America: differences in nomenclature

This book was written for the English market and, as some of the breed names vary between the UK and North America, the following list of comparative breed names should help American readers. Breeds and colors recognized in Great Britain are given on the left.

The American name is the same, *except where given*. There exist in addition certain varieties in the US which are not known in Britain, and which are therefore not featured in this book.

Great Britain	North America
Longhair	*Persian*
Black	
White (blue eyes)	
White (orange eyes)	White (copper eyes)
Blue	
Red Self	
Cream	
Smoke	
Silver Tabby	
Brown Tabby	
Red Tabby	
Chinchilla	
Tortoiseshell	
Tortoiseshell & White	Calico
Bi Colour	
Blue Cream	
Colourpoint	Himalayan
Birman	
Turkish	Turkish Van (not C.F.A.)
Self Chocolate	
Self Lilac	
Red Cameo	
Cream Cameo	
Pewter	
(U.K. – Registered with Siamese)	Balinese
(U.K. – Registered with Abyssinian)	Somali

Shorthair (British type)

The same varieties are known in the U.S.

Great Britain	North America
Foreign Shorthair	*Shorthair (Foreign type)*
Russian Blue	
Abyssinain Usual	Abyssinian Ruddy
Abyssinian Sorrel	Abyssinian Red
Burmese Brown	
Burmese Blue	Malayan Blue
Burmese Chocolate	Malayan Champagne
Burmese Lilac	Malayan Platinum
Burmese Red	
Burmese Cream	
Burmese Tortie	
Havana	Havana Brown
Foreign Lilac	Oriental Lavender
Cornish Rex	
Devon Rex	
Korat	
Foreign White	Oriental White
Foreign Black	Oriental Ebony
Foreign Blue	Oriental Blue
Oriental Spotted Tabby	
Somali Usual	Somali Ruddy
Somali Sorrel	Somali Red
Siamese	*Siamese & Colourpoint shorthair*
Seal Point	
Blue Point	
Chocolate Point	
Lilac Point	Lilac Point (Frost Point)
Tabby Point	Lynx Colourpoint shorthair
Red Point	Flame (Red) Colourpoint shorthair
Tortie Point	Tortie Colourpoint shorthair
Cream Point	Cream Colourpoint shorthair
Balinese	(U.S. – separate register)

The authors wish to acknowledge the kind help of Daphne Negus, editor of *Cat World International*, P.O. Box 35635, Phoenix, Arizona 85069, in the compilation of this material.

Contents

Acknowledgments 6
Introduction 7

1 Buying a pedigree kitten 9

Where to find a kitten; choosing a kitten; the 'papers'; neutering; inoculations; are you interested in breeding?

2 Choosing your breed 15

The Long-hair or Persian; the British Short-hair; The Foreign Short-hair; the Siamese; the Burmese

3 Introducing your kitten to its new home 51

Choosing a basket; when your kitten reaches home; nutrition; introducing the kitten to other animals; keeping the kitten amused; the kitten and the outside world; confining the kitten to your garden; the 'flat' cat; keeping in contact with your kitten's breeder

4 Caring for your cat 59

Parasites; infectious diseases; your cat's general health

Where to go for further information 63
Index 64

Acknowledgments

The authors wish to thank the following for their help in the preparation of this book:

Mrs Barbara Harrington, who typed the manuscript; Mrs Robine Pocock (Foreign Short-hairs); Rob and Val Steel (British Short-hairs); Dave Facey (Long-hairs); Graham Hunt MRCVS, BVSc (general veterinary advice).

All the photographs in this book were taken by the authors.

Published 1984 by Arco Publishing, Inc.
215 Park Avenue South, New York, NY 10003

©Paddy Cutts and Christina Payne 1981
First published 1981

All rights reserved. No part of this publication may be reproduced, in any form or by any means, without permission from the Publisher

Library of Congress Cataloging in Publication Data

Cutts, Paddy.
   Pedigree cats & kittens.

   Bibliography: p.
   Includes index.
   1. Cats. 2. Cat breeds. 3 Kittens. I. Payne, Christina. II. Title. III Title: Pedigree cats and kittens.
SF442.C88   1983   636.8   83-11938
ISBN 0-668-05949-4
ISBN 0-668-05953-2 (pbk.)

Printed in Hong Kong

Introduction

This book aims to help the first-time pedigree kitten buyer.

It outlines the different breeds available, and describes both their type and their temperament.

The mystique of the pedigree breeding world is explained, and advice given on what to look for when choosing a kitten. It takes you, step by step, through the first weeks after you bring your kitten home, and shows you how to introduce it to other pets with the minimum of fuss.

Although not intended as a feline medical handbook, it describes the common ailments to which the kitten might be prone, and how to deal with them.

We hope that you will enjoy reading this book, and that you will have many happy years of pleasure from your pedigree cat.

Chapter 1
Buying a pedigree kitten

How do you go about buying a pedigree kitten? Indeed, what breed to choose?

There are over sixty different breeds of cat, but these may be broken down into three distinct groups — the Long-hair (or Persian), the British Short-hair and the Foreign Short-hair. In type and temperament they vary considerably, and deep thought should be given to these two factors before committing yourself to sharing your life with a feline. Cats can live for over twenty years, so do not take this decision lightly!

Where to find a kitten

Pet shops and street markets will offer a showcase of appealing pets, but all too often nothing is known of their background. Often purchased *en masse* from less than discerning breeders, these kittens frequently have problems that can result in extremely costly veterinary bills. If they have been parted from their mother at a tender age, they are likely to be fearful of people and other animals, and may take a long time to settle into their new home: they may not be inoculated, making them most susceptible to any infections, many of which can prove fatal.

Many reputable pet shops will now not actually 'stock' kittens, but most will be happy to put you in contact with a discerning breeder whom they know to have good, sound and healthy stock.

A local veterinary surgeon (vet) is another good starting point: vets are often in contact with breeders, and will offer help and advice to someone seeking a new pet.

Various publications, including most national and local newspapers, have 'animals for sale' columns, but there is one specialist cat publication, *Cats* (see page 63), where a selection of different breeds will be advertised. A few telephone calls, and you will most likely find a breeder in your area who has what you want.

One of the best methods is to contact a breed or local area cat club; a list of these clubs can be obtained from the Governing Council of the Cat Fancy, generally known as the GCCF (see page 63). Many of these clubs run a 'kitten-list', and will be pleased to give you advice and put you in contact with the right breeder.

A look through *Cats* will reveal a list of forthcoming shows (this can also be obtained from the GCCF): visiting a show is an excellent way to see different breeds together, and to meet the breeders. Advertisements in the show catalogue will tell you who has stock for sale. It should be remembered, however, that kittens should never be purchased from a stranger direct from a show. Although all kittens are inspected by a 'vet' before being allowed into the show premises, there is always the chance that an illness may go undetected: wherever a number of animals are together there will be a greater risk of infection, and young animals are more susceptible than most.

Choosing a kitten

Having found a breeder, do not be put off if you are asked a lot of questions. To start with, many

British Silver Spotted with kittens

British Short-hair kittens: red, blue and smoke

Opposite Burmese kitten washing his foot

breeders have a waiting list of several months, and this is usually a good indication of sought-after stock. You will probably be asked about your home and family, and whether you have any other pets. A good breeder will invite you to look at the kittens when they are about 7-8 weeks old, and ask you to make a preliminary selection. At this point, you may be asked to leave a small deposit: this will vary, but it is usually an amount that would cover the cost of re-advertising if, for some reason, you were unable to take the kitten. Not all breeders will ask for this, but many do and it is best to be forewarned!

When you arrive to look at the kittens, ask if you can see the other adult cats. This will be a good indication as to the general health of the animals and will also show you how the kittens will be when they grow up from the point of view of both temperament and type. ('Type', incidentally, is used in the cat world to mean the particular bone structure of a breed — for example, the long nose and muzzle of the Siamese, and the short nose and broad muzzle of the Persian, or Long-hair.) The cats should be friendly and easy to handle: think twice if they seem nervous or timid...they may just be unused to strangers, but it may indicate illness, personality problems, or both.

The kittens should be bright and active, with clear eyes and clean coats. Pick them up — their tummies should be round, unbloated and soft: hardness in this region often denotes the presence of worms. They should react quickly to stimuli — throw a piece of paper, and they should pounce immediately. Look at the teeth and gums — the teeth should be clean and white, the gums pink and their breath sweet-smelling. Kittens are usually house reared, and used to people and general household hub-bub!

If all seems in order, then start to choose. You may already have a preference for a male or female: if not, ask the breeder's advice. If you are looking purely for a pet, the breeder may show you kittens that are not of show standard — their eyes may be of the wrong hue, the tail kinked, the coat colour patchy, the ears too large or too small: these kittens are perfectly healthy but are usually sold for less than the 'perfect' specimen, and their nature will still be typical of the breed. Often these faults are imperceptible to the uninitiated, but would certainly be noticed by an expert. If you do buy such a kitten, respect the breeder's stipulation that it is sold purely as a 'pet' and may not be shown or used for breeding.

The 'papers'

When you purchase a pedigree kitten you are entitled to receive its 'papers'. These consist of a pedigree of at least four generations, a registration number certifying that these details are correct provided by the GCCF, and a signed transfer form (without the last your cat cannot compete in shows or produce progeny in your name).

To protect the buying public the GCCF have enforced the rule that *all* kittens sold as 'pedigree' examples of their breed must have this documentation. Any breeder selling such stock without the 'papers' can be taken to task under the Trades Description Act! However, if at the time of sale, you agree to buy a 'pet' kitten, with obvious faults, the breeder may ask you to sign a legal document to the effect that the cat in question will be neutered, and never shown — you will still have all the papers however. This is a simple step that ensures the reputation of both the breeder, and the breed as a whole.

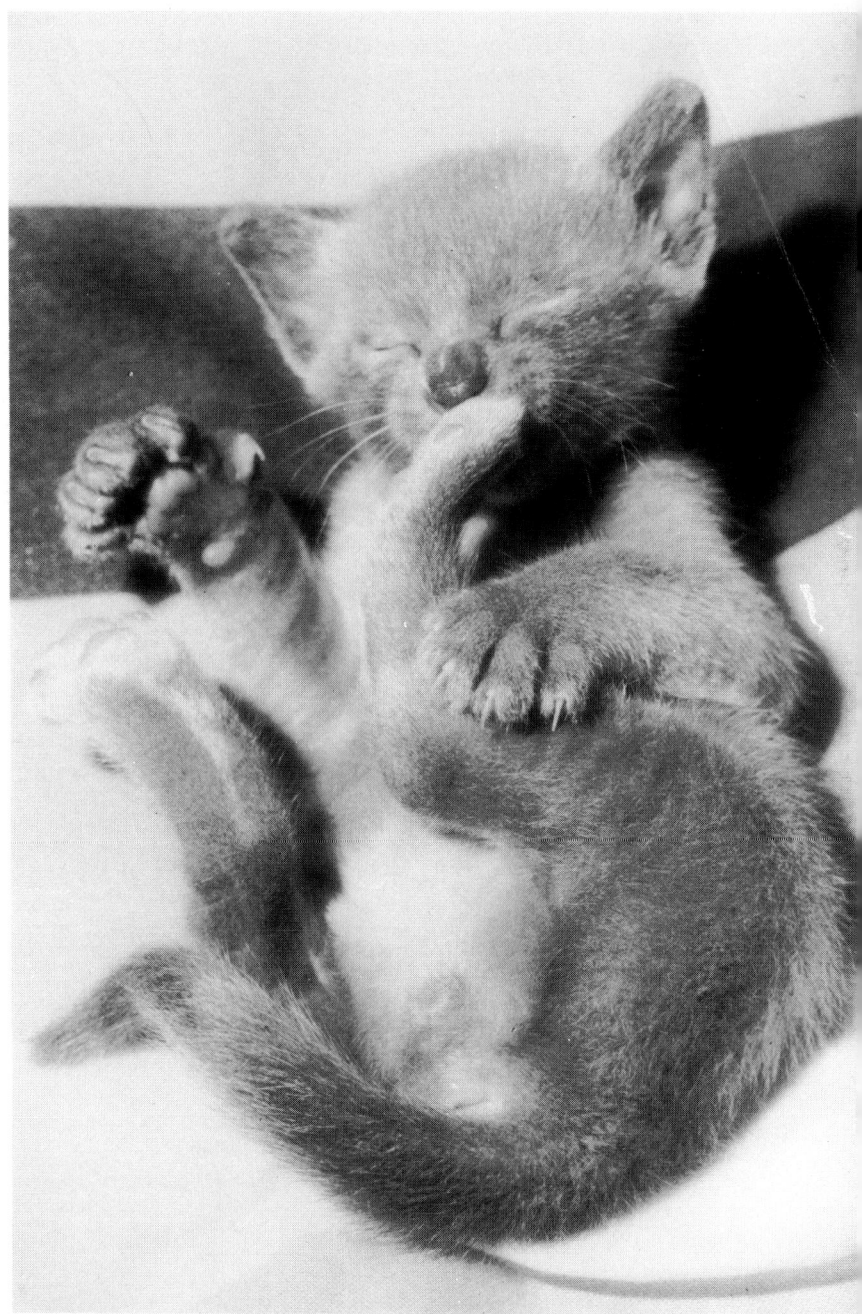

Inoculations

Whether you are taking the pick of the litter for showing, a pet kitten, or a '57-varieties' moggie, you should never take a kitten that is less than twelve weeks old, or that has not been inoculated. Kittens are at their greatest danger from viral infections between six weeks and the time that they receive their first injection. Before this they are protected by the natural antibodies found in the mother's milk, and once they are weaned they no longer have this natural immunity. It is most unfair to subject an unprotected kitten to the outside world, as many of the diseases to which it would be prone are fatal.

There are, as with dogs and other animals, vaccines that can be obtained for the various diseases. The most important vaccine is for Feline Infectious Enteritis (FIE), as this is the most lethal disease. It is not, as the name suggests, just a stomach complaint, but a virus that spreads extremely quickly and can cause death within a few days. *No kitten should be sold without the FIE inoculation.*

Cat 'flu, or Feline Viral Rhinotracheitis as it is correctly termed, may be effectively prevented by either an inoculation or a series of drops inserted into the nose; however the decision to protect against cat 'flu should be discussed with your vet who may or may not consider vaccination appropriate.

Neutering

There are born too many unwanted kittens that either lead very sad lives or are, luckily, rescued by one of the many cat charities. It is your responsibility not to add to this growing problem of unwanted kittens, and you should seriously consider the future of any kittens your cats may produce.

Therefore any kitten not intended for specific breeding purposes should be neutered at about six months of age. For a male kitten, the operation is simple and, although requiring an anaesthetic, the kitten will recover quickly. Spaying a female is a more complicated operation, and she may take a day or so to get back to normal. During this time she needs gentle handling, peace and quiet, and may show a lack of appetite.

Contrary to popular opinion, it is not cruel to have an animal neutered before it has experienced 'life'! Indeed, to use the old adage, 'What they've never had, they've never missed.' Neutered cats will NOT become fat or lazy, and the effects of the operation will curtail their otherwise normal desire to spray, fight and wander, leaving you with a most contented, happy pet.

Are you interested in breeding?

Unless you have a lot of time, and often money, to spare, it is inadvisable to consider breeding: you can gain much enjoyment from just showing your pet, and all championship shows have special classes for kittens and neuters. If, having considered the matter seriously, you decide that you would like a suitable female, or 'queen', for breeding, then ensure that you start with the very best that you can afford. Go to the cat shows, and keep an eye on the results of the breed that you are interested in. By joining the breed club, even before you have bought your kitten, you will meet helpful and experienced breeders who will be pleased to offer advice to a novice such as yourself. Having found a breeder that you like, and have confidence in, leave her to make the selection from her litter for you. Her experience will be greater than your own, and she will be able to pick the best example for you. The kitten should be good and healthy, of excellent type with no obvious faults, and with a gentle disposition. You may find that the breeder will want to keep the kitten longer, to ensure that the type is developing to the correct standard.

She may even insist that it goes to a show before you are finally allowed your new kitten.

Opposite Bi-colour Long-hair kittens

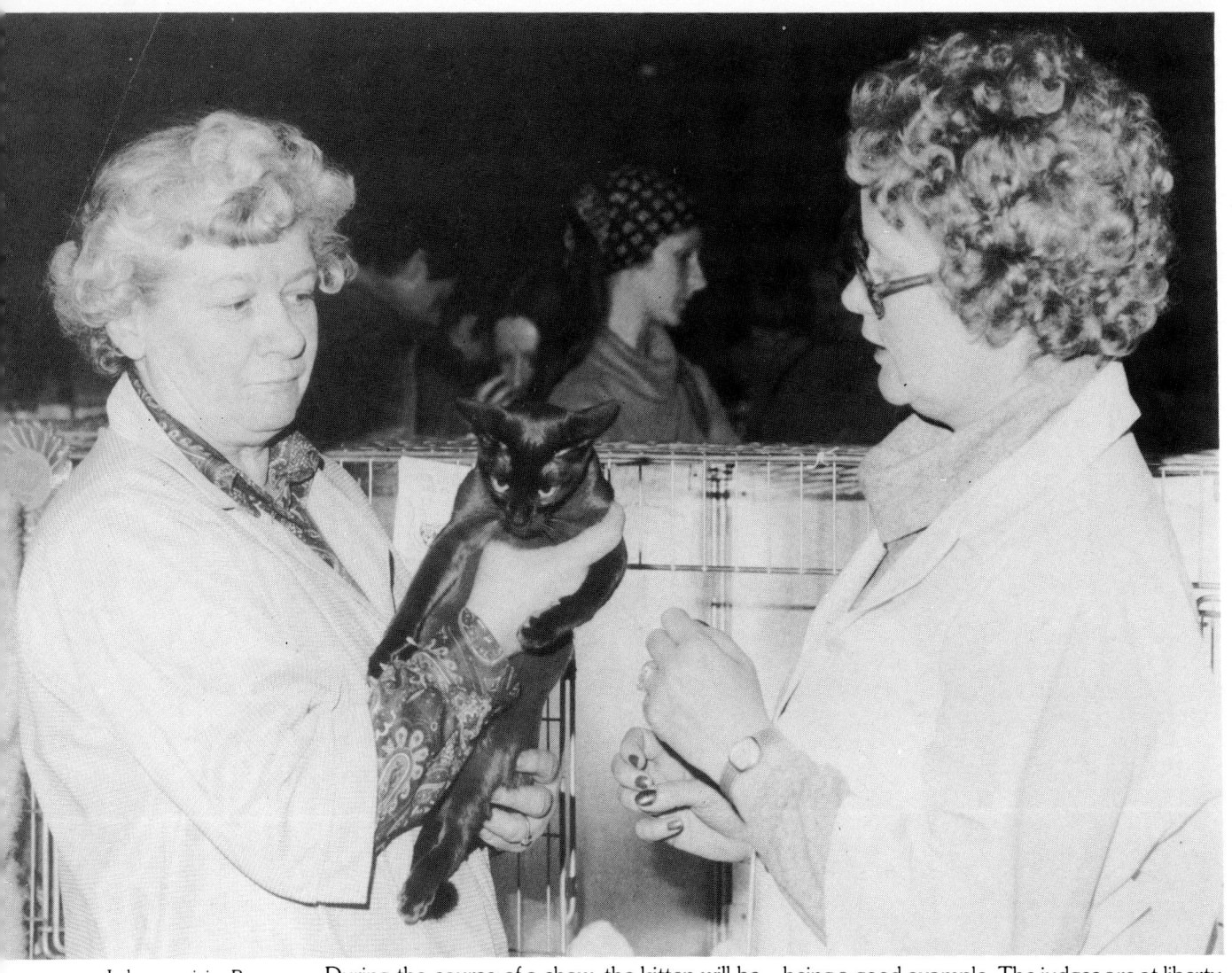

Judge examining Burmese cat at a show

During the course of a show, the kitten will be examined by several different specialists of the breed, and you will therefore have a reasonably good idea of the class and potential of your cat. If the kitten does not fare well, the breeder may suggest that you wait for another litter. Any kitten winning a 'colour' card, that is being placed 1st, 2rd, 3rd or Reserve, is usually deemed as being a good example. The judges are at liberty to withold first prizes if they feel that the exhibits are not up to standard, but in a very large class even a white 'Very Highly Commended' card can mean quite a lot! Most judges will be pleased to read their appraisal of your kitten to you, but they should never be interrupted during the busy part of their day!

Chapter 2
Choosing your breed

The Long-hair or Persian

The Long-haired cat, small and elegant with large, round expressive eyes, small, neat ears and truly luxuriant coat — what could be more beautiful? These cats have such obvious and instant appeal that they have always been popular, and are likely to remain so. Within this category are some of the most spectacular felines: film stars are often seen adorned with a Chinchilla, and these cats are frequently used in advertisements, where their grace and charm will lend an air of opulence to any surrounding.

The temperament of the Long-hair is sweet, gentle, loving and adaptable, which makes them ideal pets for anybody with a little time to set

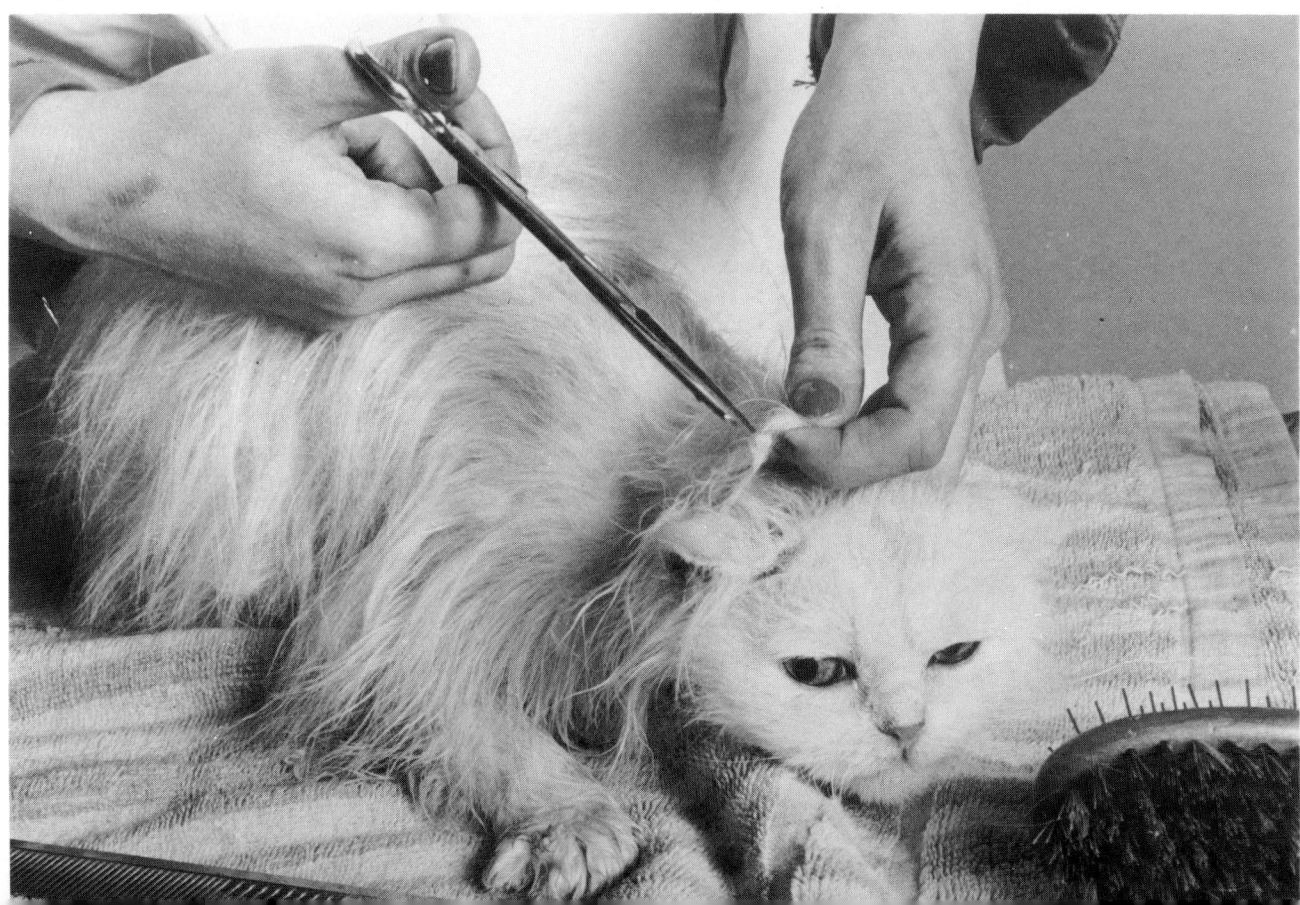

Removing matted fur from a Chinchilla

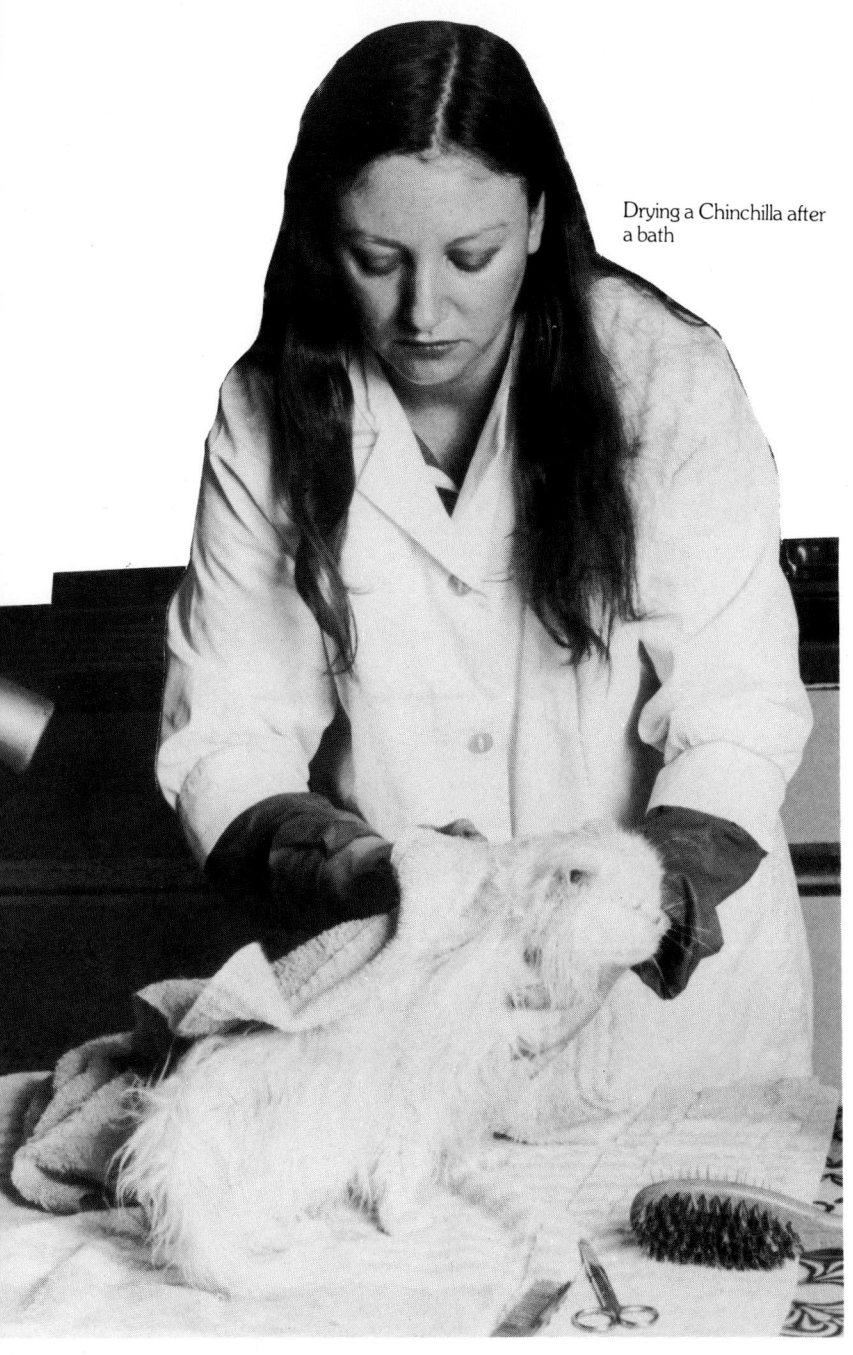

Drying a Chinchilla after a bath

aside each day for regular grooming. In good condition, and correctly groomed, the Long-hair is unsurpassable: if neglected, even for only a short time, they look more pathetic than the most lowly alley cat. The fur of the Long-hair is baby-soft and delicate, so it requires more than just an occasional brush: ten minutes a day should be enough for most cats, and it is imperative that any matted parts are completely removed. The lighter coloured cats will also need a regular shampoo to keep their pale coats sparkling, and a sprinkling of baby talcum will make the coat easier to brush and comb. Long-hairs are less vociferous than their oriental brothers: they are also less likely to wander, and do not seem to pine if left on their own. They are more likely to be content within the confines of a small area, all of these factors making them ideal pets for the city dweller.

The first Long-haired cats were imported from Angora, now known as Ankara, in Turkey, and a few years later some more were found in Persia. The latter were wider than the Turkish cats, and had slightly longer fur. The two were crossed together, and collectively became known as the Persian. The earliest known Long-hair was the Brown Tabby, which was first recorded in the mid-1800s, closely followed by the Black which was first noted in 1859 and described at the time as 'the most sought after and difficult to obtain cat'. Several breeds made their first appearance at cat shows towards the end of the nineteenth century: among these the Blue and the Chinchilla, two of the most popular colours today. The type of the early Persians was quite different to those seen today: they were much longer in the head, and with larger ears.

There are several other Long-hairs, all sharing the same type, but differing in their coat colour. The Long-haired Whites may have varying eye colour: blue, orange or 'odd' eyes, the last having one orange and one blue eye! The Tortoiseshell and Tortie-and-white are probably the most difficult types of Long-hair to breed to the correct conformation: these are 'female only' colours, in

Head study of a Blue Long-hair

Long-hairs as with all cats, and the occasional rare male that appears with this coat colour is invariably sterile. A trip to your nearest cat show will show you all the colour variations possible.

Some types of Long-hair have been produced by selective breeding programmes, one of the most notable being the Colourpoint: this is a cat with true Long-hair type, but with the coat pattern of the Siamese. It was produced in the 1950's by crossing a Blue Long-hair with a Seal-point Siamese, and now Colourpoints are to be found in as many colours as the Siamese, the most recent addition being the Tabby-point.

Within this category are two other breeds known as the 'semi-long-hairs', these being less typey than the others, and with a less dense coat. They are the Birman and the Turkish Van (not to be confused with the original cats from Angora). Birmans are known as the sacred cats of Burma, and are a truly exotic breed. Many legends surround their early history, and it is believed that when a cat dies, the soul of a priest accompanies it on the journey to Heaven. The breed was founded in France, but did not make its appearance in Britain until the 1960's. The Birman looks a little like a Colourpoint, but it is more delicate with a more pointed face and white feet. It has a wonderful temperament, being intelligent, loving and gentle, and makes a wonderful companion.

The Turkish Van, also known as the Swimming Cat, was found in the Lake Van area of Southern Turkey: it displays an affinity for water not normally regarded as a feline attribute! The coat colour should always be white, with a white blaze on the face, and auburn markings on the face and tail. The breed is strong and adaptable: the cats have large appetites and thrive on raw meat and supplementary starch foods such as brown bread and boiled rice.

Opposite Long-haired Odd-eyed White

Above Long-haired Tortoiseshell

Overleaf

Above right Tortoiseshell Long-hair

Below right Seal-point Colourpoint Long-hair

Left Tabby-point Colourpoint Long-hair

Seal-point Birman

Opposite Chocolate-point Balinese

Experimental breeds within this group include the Balinese, which has now been recognized by the GCCF. This, in essence, is a Long-haired Siamese — it has the same long, graceful type, but a long coat.

Contrary to popular opinion, the Long-hair is not a hot house plant that needs regular cosseting, and it is not a faddy eater — the only extra consideration to be given is that of grooming.

The British Short-hair

The British Short-hairs are very popular, and are one of the oldest breeds of cat. Indeed, they are Britain's native cat. They are rather similar in type to the Long-hairs, but the coat should be short and plushy like a long-piled velvet. The standards call for a compact, well muscled cat. The ears should be small and neat and set low on the head, with large, round, expressive eyes. The eye colour should be orange, with two exceptions. The White may have eye colour of orange or blue — or it may be 'odd-eyed', where there is one eye of each colour, and the Tabbies' eyes may be green or hazel. The head should be massive and round, and in profile show a good chin.

British Short-hairs make some of the best pets: they are sturdy and easy to look after. They need little in the way of grooming other than a weekly brush to remove dead hair. They are eager eaters, and will benefit from a good mixed diet. Their voices are quiet, and their temperament similar: they lack the typical 'wanderlust' of the foreign-type breeds, and are more likely to be content asleep in front of the fire. They appear not to resent confinement and make ideal companions for the flat dweller.

The British cats that we see today are the result of mating the indigenous cat of Britain with the Long-hair, and even now it is common to outcross occasionally to a Long-hair as this has been shown to improve the general type and eye colour of the breed as a whole.

Opposite British Blue kitten at play

Pair of Short-haired British White Kittens (these are Orange-eyed)

British Black

British Blue

British cats appear in many different colours, and the most popular is most probably the Blue. A somewhat darker blue than the Burmese or Russian, it is a most appealing colour and shows the deep orange eyes off to great advantage. The coat of the Blue differs slightly from those of the other British cats, and the judges today look for a definite 'plush'. British Blues should never look sleek.

The Black is another popular colour, and tales abound of these cats being involved in witchcraft — many thought them to be omens of ill fate. Although the general conformation should be that of a typical British, the coat should never be 'plush' but should be sleek and shiny with no trace of white hairs.

British Cream

The Blue-cream is probably the rarest of all, and is one that is difficult to breed. The standard calls for a perfectly mingled coat of cream and blue, with no solid patches of either colour.

The Cream is rapidly gaining popularity, and it is only since the last war that breeders have tried to improve the quality of these cats. The early Creams were very barred, patchy and spotted on the coat, but generations of careful breeding have almost eliminated these faults.

Centre British Black saying 'hello'

Right British Blue-cream

Tabby cats have always been popular and are the oldest breed known. Today, within the British section, they are available in many colours. One of the most popular is the Silver Tabby: they have particularly attractive markings and sweetly expressive faces. As a general rule they are more dainty than the other types of British cat.

Within the general British section falls the Manx, one of the oldest breeds of cat and traditionally found on the Isle of Man. Although they can be of any colour, the tail must be completely absent with no vestige left behind. Manx with a slight lump at the base of the spine are known as 'stumpies' and 'rumpies' and these are unable to compete at cat shows.

British Red Tabby at a show

Left Silver Tabby British Short-hair kitten at play

The Foreign Short-hair

This group also includes the Siamese and Burmese, which are dealt with separately. Included here are the Abyssinians, Russian Blues, Havana, Devon and Cornish Rex, Korat and the Foreign White, Black, Lilac and Blue, and the Oriental Tabby. They all differ in type, but are generally a complete contrast with the British Short-hair and the Long-hair. The Foreign varieties have wedge-shaped faces, fairly large pricked ears, almond-shape eyes, long graceful bodies on tall, slim legs, and long tapering tails: they should never be massive cats.

They all enjoy human companionship and dislike being left on their own for long periods, and are usually happier if they have another cat for company. Many of them tend to be quite vocal, and will enjoy having a conversation with you! Generally they are far more intelligent than the British Short-hairs and Long-hairs: they are the original 'curious' cat, and will be into anything and everything. They are not a breed to be chosen by the faint hearted!

Abyssinian
This is essentially a graceful and elegant cat, closely resembling the cats portrayed in the murals and statuettes of the ancient Egyptians. The ancestors of the Abyssinian were mummified, and given ceremonial burials. They have also often been nick-named the 'bunny' cat, as their coat has an appearance similar to that of the wild British rabbit.

The first Abyssinian seen in England was called Zula, and was brought to this country from Ethiopia in 1868. They were recognized in England in 1882, and were later introduced to America in 1909. The standard calls for a medium-sized cat, never large or coarse, with a tail that is broader at the base and not so whip-like as the Siamese. The Abyssinian fur is ticked, that is to say each hair has two or three bands of

Left Abyssinian kittens: left, Normal; right, Lilac

Red (now known as Sorrel) Abyssinian

Two Russian Blue kittens

Opposite Russian Blue

colour ending in black at the tip. The colour for the normal Abyssinian should be a rich ruddy brown ticked with black, and the underparts should harmonize, preferably being orange-brown. This subtle colouring gives the cat a 'glowing' look.

In 1963 the Red, now known as the Sorrel, Abyssinian was recognized in Britain. With the same type, they differ only in coat colour, which should be a rich copper red, ticked with the darker colours. Although there are more colours today, such as the blue, lilac and chocolate, it is only the usual and the sorrel that have been granted championship status by the GCCF in Britain.

Russian Blue

These cats were first seen at a cat show in 1880, and considerable argument ensued as to the correct type and colour. Unfortunately they were subjected to much indiscriminate breeding in the early years, and many breeders used cats

with British type, making it difficult to distinguish between the Russian Blue, and the British varieties. During the early 1900's breeders tried to establish the Russian on a firmer footing, but encountered setbacks during the Second World War when the breed was mated with Siamese, resulting in the appearance of many faults. Even the Russian Cat Club, seeing little future in the breed, was dissolved. However, a small group of breeders keen to re-establish the Russian, introduced a very strict breeding programme, which was eventually accepted by the GCCF. It was thanks to these post-war breeders that we now have a Russian with the correct type and colour.

The Russian today has a silver-blue coat that is short and fine, giving an almost seal-like appearance: it should be so thick and luxuriant that the skin is not visible underneath. They have almond-shaped eyes, with vivid green colouring and set rather wide apart. The head should be wedge-shaped with a straight profile from head to nose. The ears should be large and set well apart, showing a flat skull.

The Russians are gaining in popularity constantly, and they make fine companions: they are probably the quietest of all the foreign cats, being rather shy, and they hardly ever use their voices. They are very loving, and will become very attached to their owners, displaying all their love and affection to the people they trust.

Rex, Cornish and Devon

These fascinating cats are instantly recognizable by their wavy or curly coat, which has often earned them the nick-name of the 'poodle' cat. The coat is the result of a natural mutation that has produced a change in the basic structure of the hairs.

Although the cats' appearance is striking in itself, it is the personality of the Rex that has drawn people to them. They really are the clowns of the cat world: they are, like all foreign cats, very intelligent, but the Rex are extroverts, abounding with love and affection. One interesting point that should be noted is that the Rex fur, unlike other cats' fur, does not cause an allergy with asthmatics, and these little cats are usually the only cats that can live happily with a person suffering from this complaint.

The Rex was first seen in 1950, when, amongst a litter of normal-coated farm cats, a curly-coated kitten was discovered. This kitten was mated back to his mother, producing more curly-coated kittens in her next litter. This new breed was called the Rex because of the similarity to the Asrex rabbit, and later the Cornish Rex, because these first kittens were discovered on Bodmin Moor in Cornwall. A

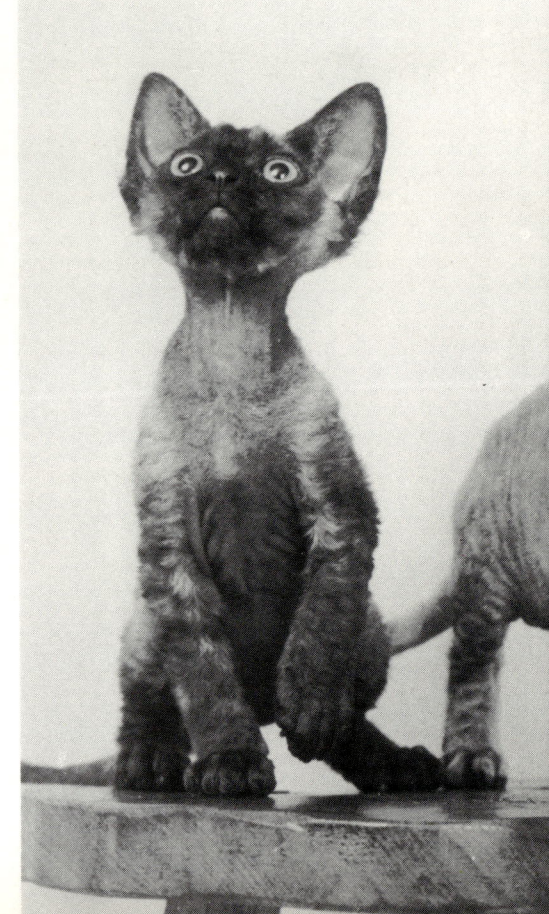

White Devon Rex

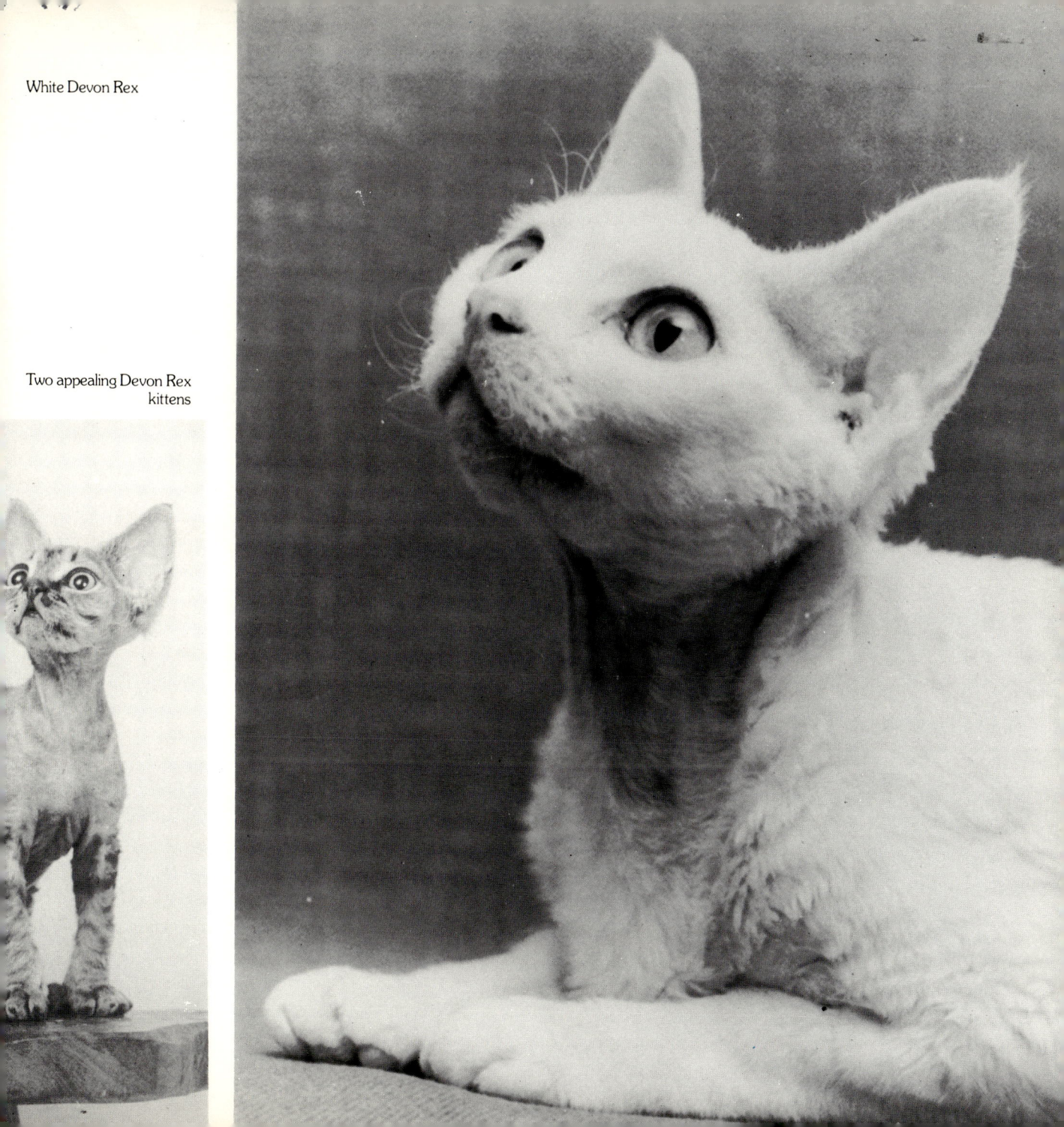

Two appealing Devon Rex kittens

Red Cornish Rex

'Tortie' Devon Rex

detailed breeding programme was undertaken to outcross these first litters, using Burmese and British Short-hairs.

In 1960 another male curly-coated kitten was found, this time near a tin mine in Devon. This kitten, although having a curly coat, was found to differ in type and size from the first Rex found, and was subsequently known as the Devon Rex.

All the Rex have definite foreign type: the Devon has a short wedge head, with clearly defined stop, full cheeks, and low-set, wide-based ears, giving a somewhat 'pixieish' face. The coat is wavy, rather than curly. The Cornish has a medium-to-long head, and the coat is short and dense with a tendency to curl. Any coat colour can be 'rexed', and through recent breeding programmes a Si-Rex has been produced, giving the full Rex coat but with Siamese markings.

Korat

This breed originates from Thailand, and it is highly regarded by the Thai people, as they believe that the cat will bring good fortune. These cats, although popular in the USA and Canada, are comparatively rare in England. They are recognized by the GCCF in Britain but have not as yet been granted Championship status.

The Korat has a self-coloured coat, which should be a definite blue all over, tipped with silver, giving a silvery sheen. It is a muscular, medium sized cat, with a heart-shaped face. The tail is medium in length, with a rounded tip, and the coat texture should be glossy and close lying. Korats make fine, companionable pets, being quiet and gentle, but playful.

Havana

This is a man-made breed, originating from the Siamese. It is a chestnut-brown colour, but without any of the distinctive Siamese 'pointing', and with green eyes.

The breed was recognized in Britain in 1958, and Havanas are now very popular. The kittens are most attractive, with a soft downy fur of a rich chestnut brown: they are 'self' colour cats and, unlike the Brown Burmese, they are born with the same coat colour that they have when adult. Their personality is very similar to that of the Siamese, making them exceptionally lively and loving, with loud voices.

Oriental Tabbies and Spotteds

These are a recent addition to the Foreign breeds, and they have recently been granted Championship status by the GCCF in Britain. They are also derived from original Siamese stock and have similar characteristics.

Apart from their natural inquisitiveness, all the Foreign cats are adaptable and make ideal pets. They need little in the way of special attention, and most will only require the minimum of grooming: usually an occasional brush followed by a polish up with velvet or chamois leather.

Overleaf
Left Havana

Right Foreign White

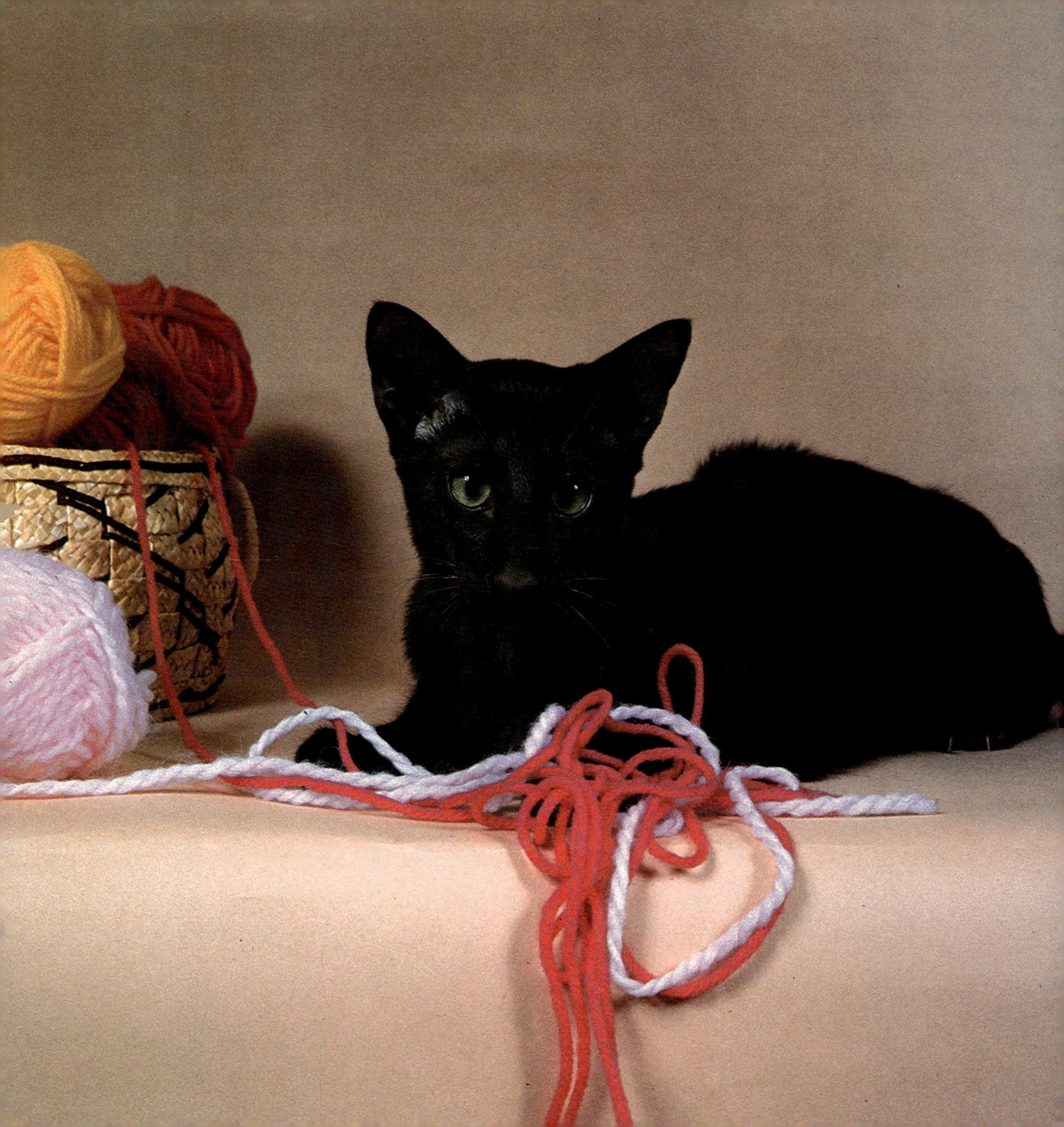

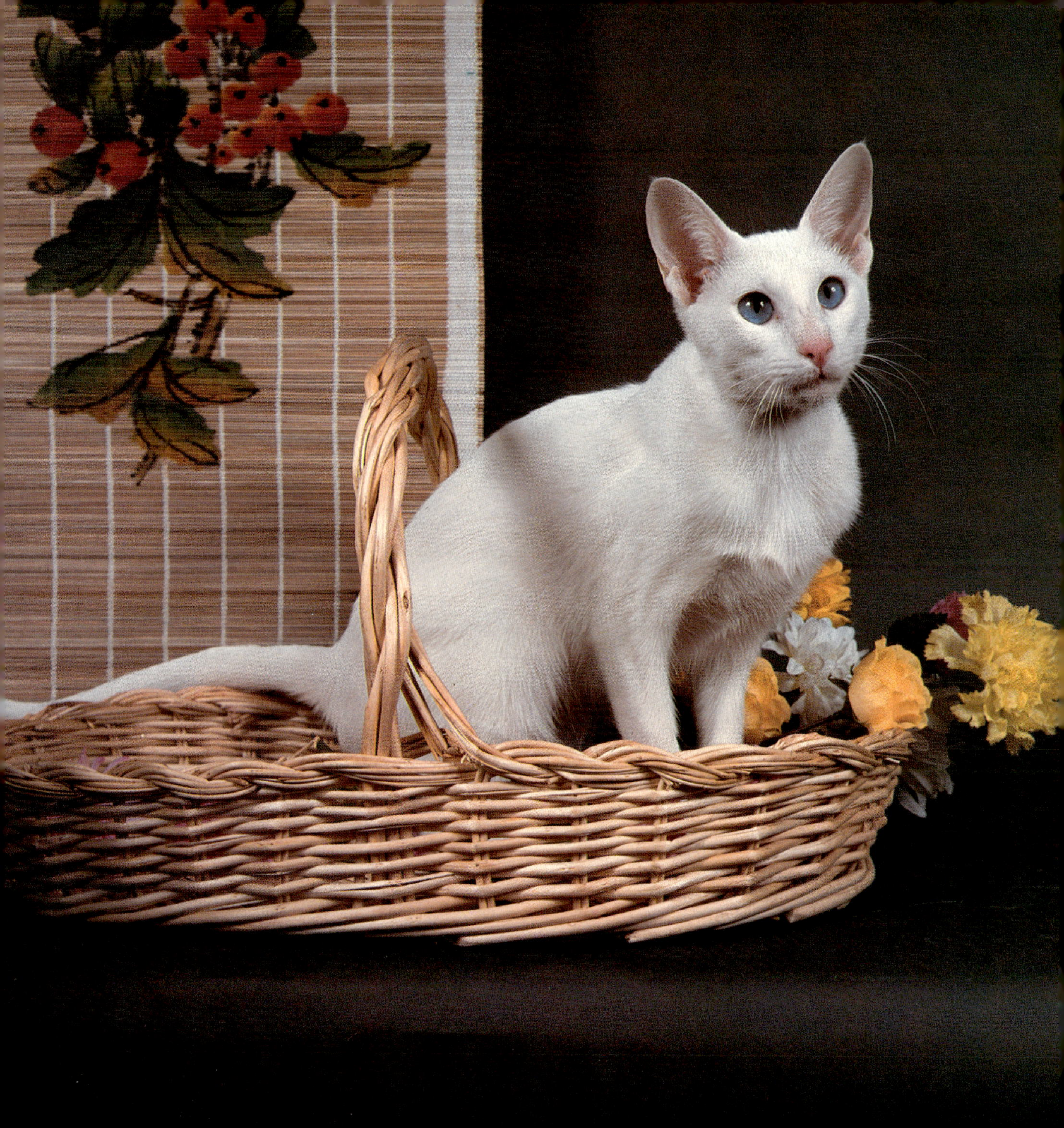

Siamese trying to steal the dinner

Opposite Seal-point Siamese

Foreign White, Black, Lilac and Blue
These cats are, in essence, solid coated Siamese and all are recognized by the GCCF: the Foreign Blue, however, has not yet been granted championship status. As with the Havana, their temperament and personality is indistinguishable from that typical of the Siamese, and they all make intelligent and amusing pets.

The Siamese

Siamese are probably the most instantly recognizable breed of pedigree cat, and one of the most popular.

Siamese make wonderful pets, and possess a larger than life quality that leaves you in no doubt about their personality. Often they will attach themselves to one human owner, displaying great affection and loyalty. A healthy Siamese at play will romp with you for hours, and even in more stately adulthood, they will continue with their fascinating antics. No other cat can surpass the Siamese for intelligence: opening doors and windows presents no problem, and the stealing of the Sunday lunch can become a familiar pastime! The Siamese voice is unmistakable: it is certainly not a quiet breed of cat, and the voice can be irksome to neighbours — however, it is usually accepted by the owner as an obvious conversation piece.

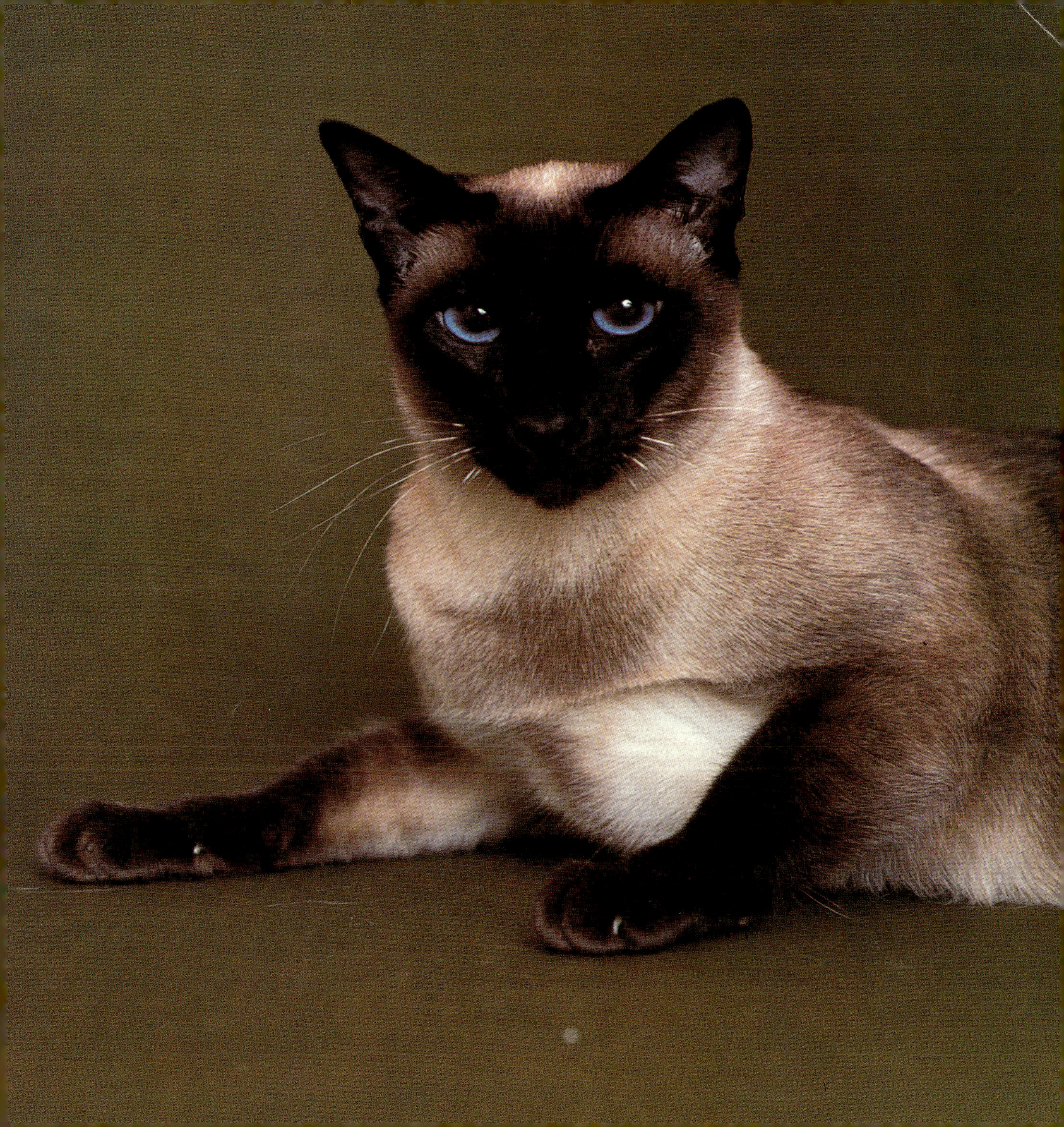

Chocolate-point
Siamese

Siamese will happily train to a lead or harness, allowing both cat and human to travel places together, the cat exploring and enjoying every moment.

There are many delightful legends surrounding the history of the Siamese, some of which are difficult to identify as fact or fiction! The accepted history states that the first pair of Siamese were given to the Consul-General of Siam, a Mr Gould, who brought the pair back to England in 1884, and subsequently bred from them. The progeny were shown for the first time at the Crystal Palace show in 1885. This story has been questioned by some, as other Siamese were present in England at the time, and in the limited period since it would have been impossible for all Siamese to have emanated from this one source!

It is possible that the whole truth will never be known but, because of the vague beginnings of the Siamese, some wonderful stories have evolved. It is said, for example, that they were the Royal cats of Siam, and the guardians of the Buddhist temples in Bangkok. Tales of them being smuggled out of Siam are rife, as the King of Siam was extremely jealous of his beautiful cats, and any thief would have to face dire consequences! As he would not allow any of them to be exported, it is thought that he must have given Mr Gould special permission, to bring his pair back to England.

The early cats had blue eyes, often squinting, and long tails that were prone to 'kinks'. Although squints and tail defects are considered a serious fault on the show bench today, and for the most part have been bred out completely, there are some amusing folk-stories that have evolved.

One story has it that the blue eye colouring is a gift from heaven for safely guarding the Buddhist temples.

The squint has been explained as follows. Two cats travelled into the jungle to search for a Royal goblet that had disappeared from a Temple. When the cats eventually found the treasure, it was decided that one of them, the male, should go back to the city to tell the priests of their discovery. Whilst the male cat was away, the female remained behind to guard the goblet, but stared so hard at it to ensure it's safety that she developed a squint! She became very weary, and eventually fell asleep, but curled her tail around the goblet for safekeeping. When the male cat and the priest returned, they found that she had given birth to kittens, all of them with squints and kinked tails!

Another tale explaining the kink includes the Princess of Siam who, it is said, always hung her precious rings on her cat's tail: one day the rings fell off, so she tied a knot in the cat's tail to prevent this ever happening again!

The Siamese Cat Club was first formed in 1901, and by the following year had thirty-one members: by this time a 'standard of points' had been established. The early Siamese bore little resemblance to the cats on show today: they were shorter and stockier than the long, elegant cat that we now know. The standards have been revised over the years, and now call for a cat that is:

'Medium in size, body long and svelte, legs proportionately slim, hind legs slightly longer than the front legs. Feet small and oval, tail long and tapering, straight or slightly kinked at the extremity. Head long and well proportioned, with width between the eyes narrowing in a perfectly straight line to a fine muzzle. Ears rather large and pricked wide at base. The body, legs, feet, head and tail all in proportion giving the whole a well-balanced proportion. Eyes oriental in shape and slanting towards the nose'.

Regardless of colour, the general type should conform to the above standards. The original Siamese were Seal-points, that is a dark brown on the ears, face, paws and tail, with a pale cream colour for the rest of the body. As a result of greater knowledge of genetics and careful breeding, there are now many point colours that can be found: seal, blue, chocolate, lilac, red, cream, tabby and tortie. However, whatever the colour, the cat is always, in essence, the Siamese.

The Burmese

Burmese are probably the most popular breed of short-haired cat in Britain today. They are often compared to the Siamese, their nearest oriental relative, but this comparison is really unfair as there are great differences in both type and temperament.

There are legends surrounding the Burmese cats' status in Burma, and they share with the Siamese and Birmans the tradition of having been sacred cats on guard in Buddhist temples.

The Burmese breed was established in America in the 1930's, when an original 'brown' cat was imported from Burma. This cat, a female called 'Wong Mau', intrigued the Americans, and she appeared to be in many ways similar to a Seal-point Siamese. A group of geneticists and scientists, with the help of breeders, undertook a successful breeding programme proving that the genetic make up of the Burmese was, in fact, different from that of the Siamese.

The Burmese first appeared in Britain in the late 1940's, and were shown shortly afterwards at a Cat Show in 1949. Until 1953 only the Brown Burmese had existed, but in that year a sole Blue Burmese was born. This birth caused great interest and excitement, and implied that other colours might be genetically possible. From America came the Champagne and Platinum Burmese, called Chocolate and Lilac in Britain. In Britain, breeders undertook a programme to produce Red and Cream Burmese, and the 'Tortie'. The Tortie, mated to the Chocolates and Lilacs, opened up a whole spectrum of Burmese colours, and it is now possible to have Burmese in brown, blue, chocolate, lilac, red, cream, brown tortie, blue tortie, chocolate tortie and lilac tortie.

The Burmese, irrespective of coat colour, should always follow the following standard. The body should be of medium length, hard and muscular, with a strong chest, rounded in profile. Legs should be slender in proportion to the body, the hind legs slightly longer than the front. The paws should be oval in shape. The tail should be straight and of medium length, slightly tapering to a rounded tip without any bone defect. The top of the head should be rounded, with a pronounced dome and good width between the ears, the cheek bones tapering to a short blunt wedge. In profile, the ears should have a slight forward tilt, and there should be a distinct nose break and a strong lower jaw. The eyes may be any shade of yellow, but never almond green, and should not be round in shape, the coat should be short and fine, satin-like in texture and close-lying to the body, a glossy coat being indicative of good health.

The Burmese cat is a highly intelligent, athletic, loyal and loving companion, much quieter than the Siamese, although it will 'chat' with you. To own a Burmese is to enjoy a wonderful relationship between human and feline: it will play with you and for you, defy you occasionally, and sometimes outwit you. Retrieving is one of their favourite pastimes and, as they bring back their toys time and time again, you will start to wonder if you really have a dog and not a cat at all! Because of this habit, the early Burmese were often known as the 'Dog-Cat'.

The Burmese are very sturdy and brave: they will hold their own against much larger animals, showing no fear or trepidation. They are also extremely loving, and, when exhausted with play, will curl up on your lap or shoulders and sleep for hours. They are very 'social' cats, and will pine if left confined without any company. Few breeders will sell a single Burmese if they know that it will be left alone while the owner is at work: two are much more fun, and will also be much more contented cats.

Burmese need little in the way of special care and grooming: an occasional brush, and a polish with a chamois leather are all that they require. They are not usually faddy eaters and will happily eat what is put in front of them.

Red Burmese

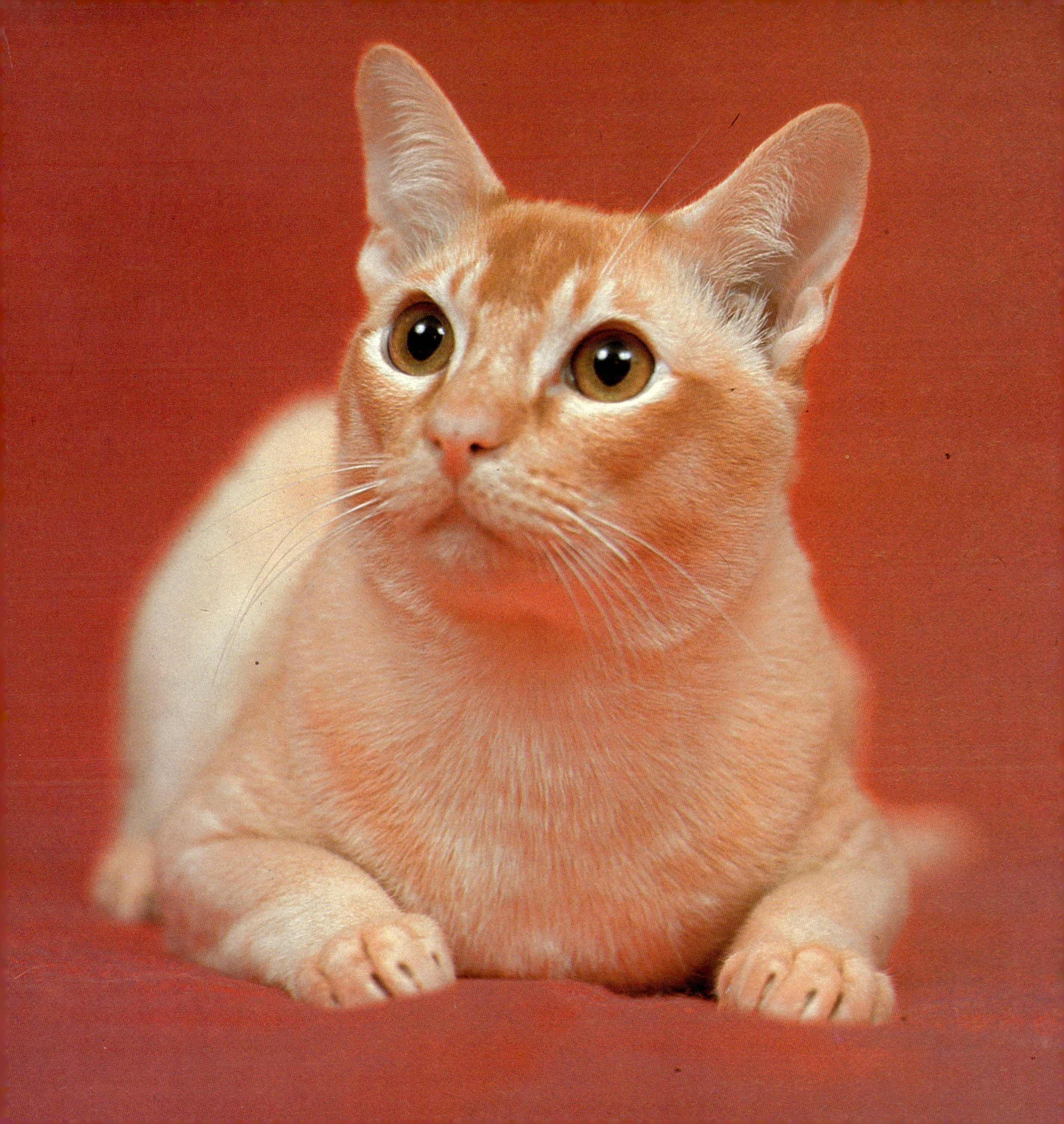

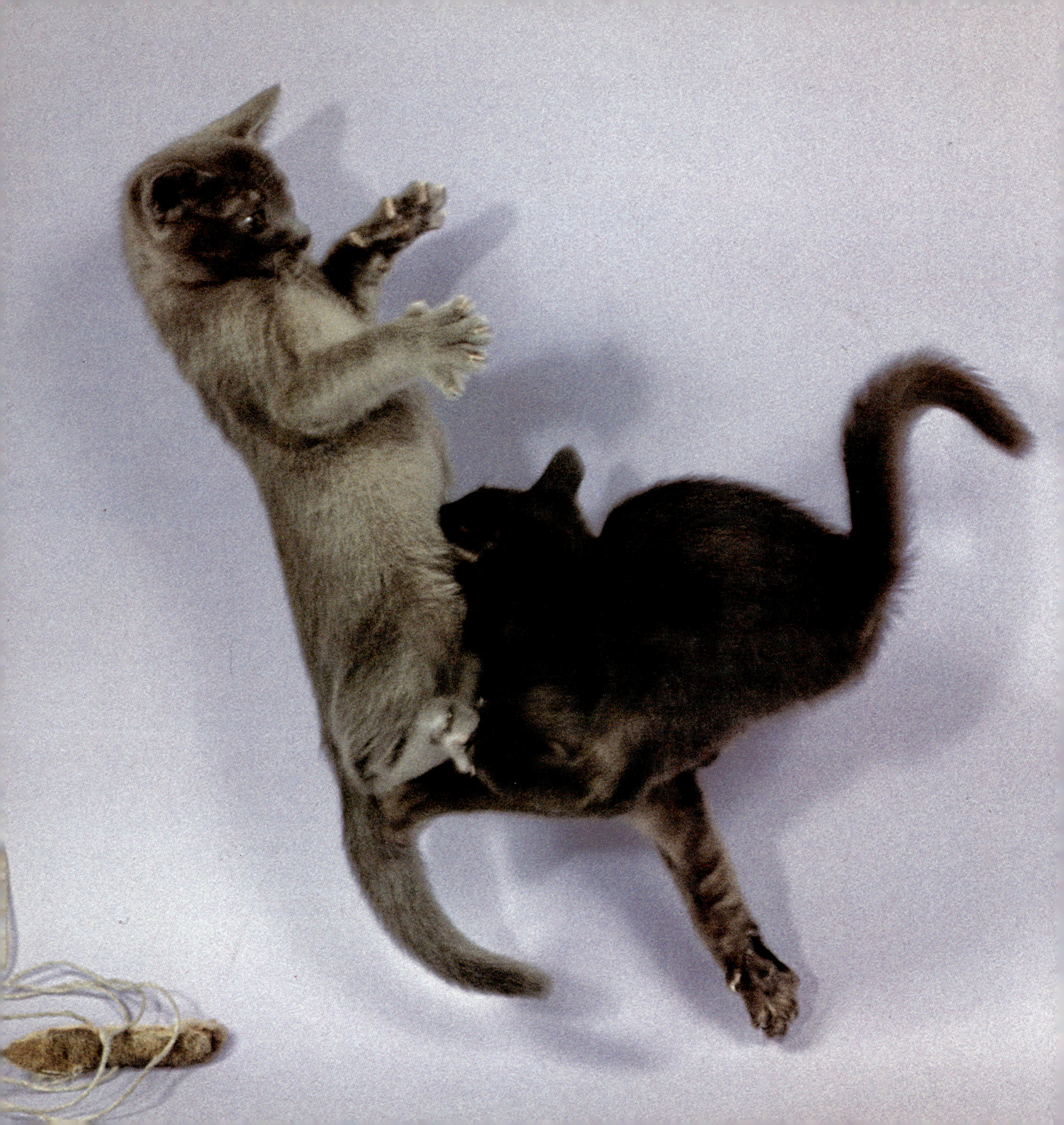

Left Brown and Blue Burmese kittens having rugby practice

Chocolate Burmese (known in America as Champagne Burmese)

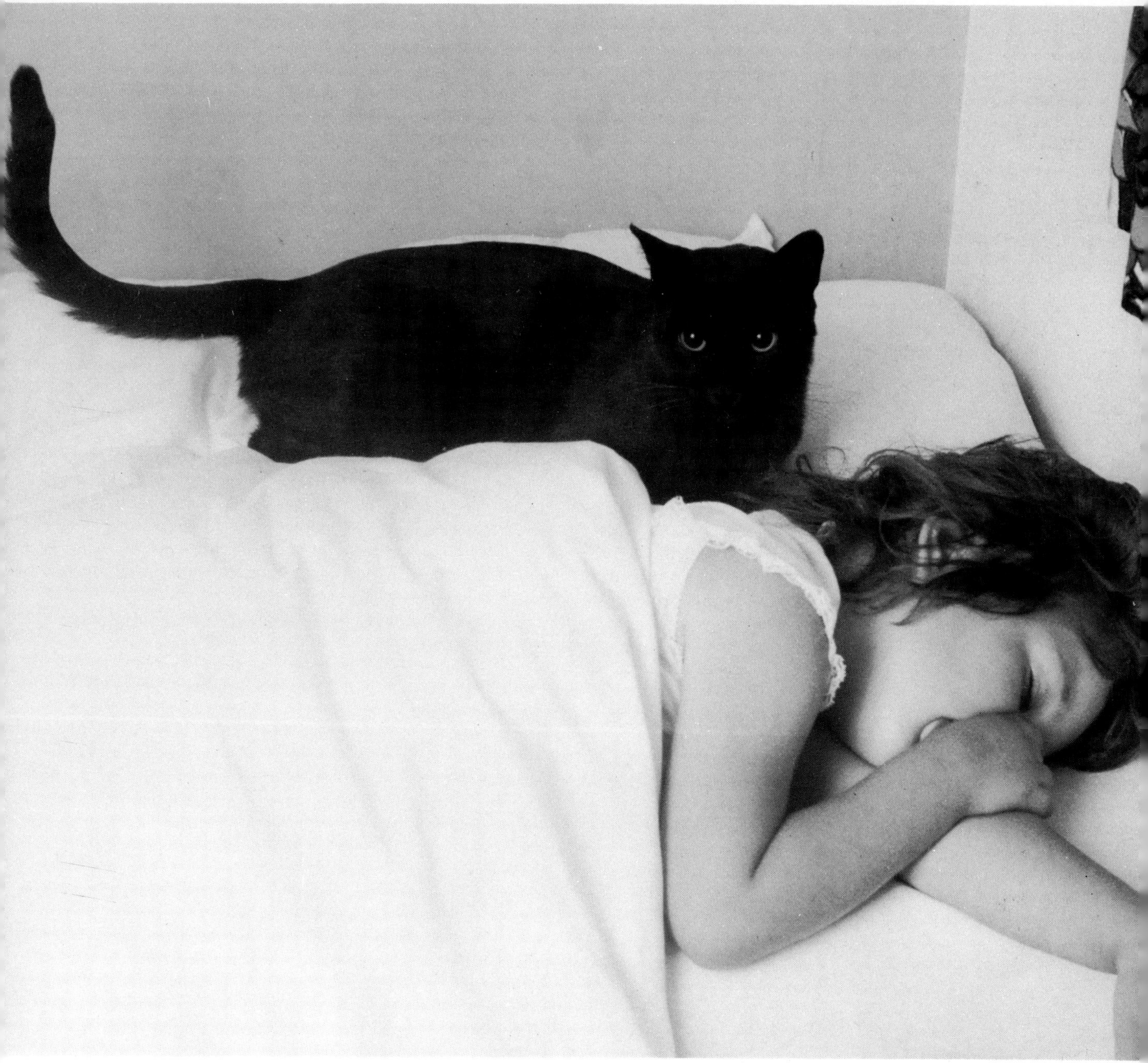

Chapter 3
Introducing your kitten to its new home

When you collect your kitten from the breeder, be sure to take a basket and blanket with you. Although old enough to leave mother, the kitten will be embarking on a journey to a new home that may cause a certain amount of distress and alarm. Kittens are usually much happier to travel in a basket, as the confinement and darkness provide them with a sense of security. Your kitten may never have been in a car before, and if it is allowed to run free, or even held in someone's arms, the experience could well be terrifying for both the kitten and yourself: few things are more nerve-wracking than a kitten under the brake pedal!

Choosing a basket

A basket is one of the most essential pieces of 'cat' equipment, but one that many new owners overlook. You will have occasion to travel with your cat at some time, perhaps to the vet, or to a boarding cattery when you go on holiday: it is most unfair to these people to take a cat loose, as there is always a danger of escape unless the cat is properly confined. For an emergency, cardboard boxes are available very cheaply at most pet shops, but most self-respecting felines will eat their way out of these with no trouble at all! Instead, invest in something more substantial: the traditional wicker baskets are very good, and strong, allowing plenty of air to circulate in the summer. They can, however, tend to be a bit draughty in the winter, unless the lower part is covered with strong paper. Very similar to this is the type made of plastic-covered wire mesh, but it has the added benefit that the cat can see what is going on outside: however, these baskets do need covering in wet weather, and a warm, insulating cover in winter.

Various new ideas for baskets are now available. There is one that resembles a zip-topped shopping bag, but with clear panels at both ends and ample ventilating holes. Containers made from domed perspex with wooden bases are proving popular, as they are extremely secure, warm, and allow the occupant virtually a 360 degree field of vision! Their only drawback is that they do tend to get very hot on long journeys in the summer months, especially for the long-haired cats. Glass-fibre containers offer security, warmth, and ventilation, and they are also extremely light and easy to clean.

When your kitten reaches home

There will probably be great excitement when you arrive home with the new kitten, and any children will want to cuddle and make a great fuss of it. The kitten may well be bewildered and confused after its journey, and too many people around it will only make matters worse. Explain to the children that for the first day or two, puss should be left alone to settle in. The kitten should be confined to one room at a time, and given ample opportunity to explore.

Make sure that it has everything that it needs, clean litter tray, water, food and a comfortable place to sleep. Cat litter can be obtained from most pet shops and supermarkets, but try to use

Cats love to sleep in bed, but this is not to be recommended with very young children or babies

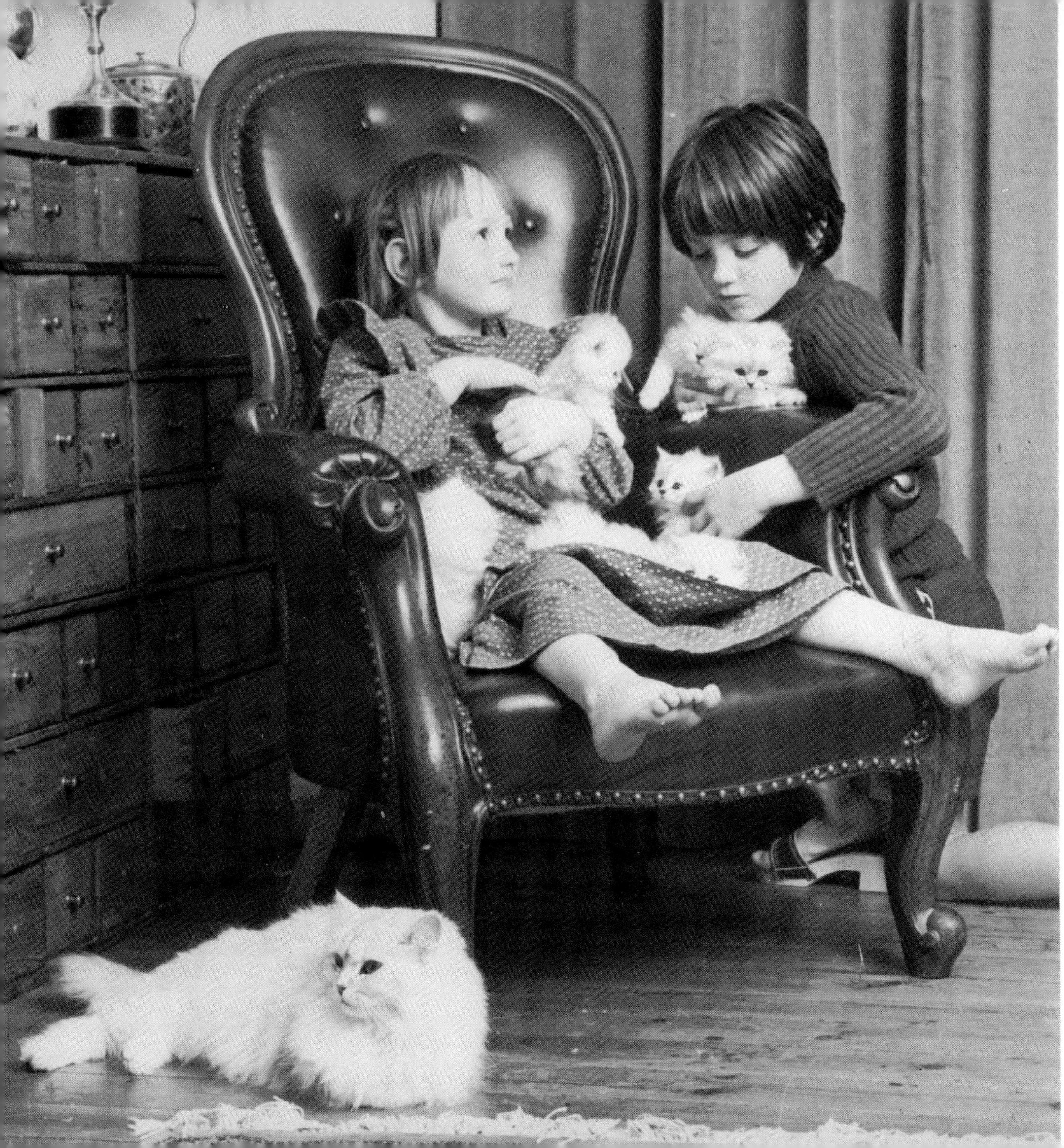

Kittens do not normally need to be toilet-trained

the brand that it has been used to, at least for the first few weeks. The tray should be changed daily, and washed and disinfected between changes. Do not use any disinfectants that contain phenols or cresols, as these are extremely poisonous to cats, and traces can be absorbed through the pads on the paws. Ammonium-based or Hypochlorite disinfectants are safe when made up to the manufacturers' recommended concentrations: if you are in any doubt, then ask your vet before using any of them.

Unlike puppies, kittens do not need to be 'house-trained': cats are the most fastidious creatures, and their toilet-training will have been given by their mother as soon as they are old enough to eat. Accidents rarely happen unless the kitten is unable to find the tray, is poorly, or finds that the tray is badly soiled: cats are so clean, that they will not use very dirty trays, so it really is important both to you and your kitten that the litter area is always clean and hygienic. If your kitten is to be a 'free range' pet, then eventually you will be able to dispense with the litter, and with a little encouragement, the cat will start to use the garden.

Opposite Teach children to handle kittens gently

These Rex kittens do not seem to lack appetite

Nutrition

The kitten may refuse food on the first day at a new home, but this is no cause for alarm! It is quite normal and due to the confusion of moving home. Most kittens, however, settle in quickly, and will soon be demanding food! As long as the kitten is fit and active, the loss of appetite is no reason to worry, but if it continues for more than 48 hours your vet should make an examination.

Although kittens have great appetites, their tummies are very small, so until six months of age they should be given four small meals a day. They grow rapidly during these first few months, and need plenty of protein. Cats are carnivores, and obtain their protein from meat. The breeder should have given you a 'diet sheet' to help you over the first few months, and this should be adhered to as far as possible. Cooked chicken and rabbit with the bones removed, are popular, as are raw red meats such as steak, heart and kidney, but these should always be offered either chopped or minced. Liver, although highly nutritious, can cause diarrhoea if given too often. When feeding your kitten raw meat, be careful not to use any meat from dubious sources, and only use really fresh meat *suitable for human consumption*. Tinned cat food is convenient and good, as it contains special formulae in a correct balance especially for cats: there is even a proprietary brand of 'kitten food' now on the market, and this is a special mixture for kittens up to nine months of age. Dried cat food is best given as a treat or a snack, and should not be used to form the main basis of a diet: it is useful if the kitten is to be left for any period of time, and it will not 'go off', but it should *always* be given with an ample supply of fresh water. Cats, in general, love fish and, provided it has been well filleted, it will give you a very pleased and contented cat! It should be remembered that fish should never be given raw. Coley, cod, and whitebait are among the favourite fresh fish, and tinned fish such as pilchards are very nutritious too. Cereal, such as cornflakes, may be mixed with fish, to provide extra roughage, but should not be mixed with meat as this can cause a souring in the stomach.

Until the kitten is about six months old, it will still need one milky feed a day: cow's milk may cause diarrhoea, and contain too much water to be used as a food. Evaporated milk and tinned rice puddings are better, or you can use powdered human baby feeds making them up a little stronger than recommended, adding in some cereal or rusk. By feeding your kitten a varied diet of tinned food, fresh meat, chicken, rabbit, fish, and cereal, you will be ensuring that it gets all the protein, vitamins, carbohydrates and roughage that it needs to grow strong and healthy: it will also be less likely to become a faddy eater when older.

After six months the diet should be reduced to three meals a day; at about one year old, when the kitten is fully grown, two meals will be enough, although snack 'treats' are always welcome!

Introducing the kitten to other animals

If you have other pets keep them away at first, and introduce them to your new kitten gently, always being present yourself. The established pets will probably resent the 'intruder', and there may well be fights. During the settling in period be sure to give the other pets plenty of fuss and love: all animals are sensitive, and they may be jealous and unhappy if you give all of your time to the new kitten, without reassuring them that they are still much loved and wanted. Fortunately, this settling in period doesn't normally last very long: sometimes it can be all over in a few hours. A battle may continue for many weeks, but it is usually only a couple of days before the animals will all be playing together.

Keeping the kitten amused

Very soon the kitten will be playing and exploring everything and anything with great interest, and will appreciate some toys to keep it amused. Some breeds, such as the Burmese and Siamese, often love retrieving and will bring back their toys time and time again for you to throw! A glance at the pet shop will reveal a great selection of toys that can be bought, and some of the most successful are those that are stuffed with cat-nip, a herb that cats adore. Ping-pong balls, filled with

A 'play-pole' will give your kitten exercise

Burmese kittens up to mischief

rice or something similar, and attached to a piece of elastic, will bring out the ballet-dancer in your kitten and you will see it perform a spectacular series of jumps, leaps and turns! A cat-scratching post is a good idea, and will save your furniture and carpets from being used as 'claw-sharpeners'. They can be purchased from pet shops, but are easily constructed at home. You will need a piece of 2 in × 2 in wood, about three feet long, and two pieces of blockboard or chipboard 18 in × 18 in. Using one piece as the base, and the other as a platform on the top, cover the whole thing with old carpet. If some toys on a piece of elastic are attached to the platform, you will provide both your kitten and yourself with great amusement, as puss will scrabble up this constantly, biffing its toys with great bravado.

The kitten and the outside world

As your kitten becomes part of the household, you will probably want to let it out into the garden to play. This is fine, but at first all playtimes should be supervised: it may get lost or stuck up a tree until it is sure of the local geography!

Do not let your cat stay out all night: it is a fallacy to think that cats want to roam at night... they don't, and they are exposed to many more dangers at night than during the daytime.

The greatest danger to a roaming kitten is the motor-car: more kittens are killed on the road each year than by disease. They have absolutely no road sense, or fear of the unknown, and may dart across the road without warning, giving the motorist little or no chance to avoid an accident. Kittens are most vulnerable up to a year old, and tend to acquire a certain amount of caution with maturity. Kittens learn caution with experience, and have long memories for an unpleasant incident: this can be used to try to teach a kitten fear of the motor-car! Place your kitten under your car, then switch on, revving very hard, sounding the horn, and generally making as

Training a cat to harness and lead

much noise as possible, but without actually letting the car move: hopefully, this will frighten the kitten enough for it to remember that the car is a most unpleasant creature!

A less traumatic way to allow your kitten fresh air, is to train it to a harness and lead, as young as possible. Cats, especially the foreign breeds, tend to take to this quite happily, allowing you to take the cat for a walk in relative safety when you and your family want to go out.

Confining the kitten to your garden

There are two ways to allow your kitten access to the garden and fresh air, but without letting it wander far. There are several purpose built 'cat houses' that can be purchased and, depending on the amount of space you have available, considerably large runs can be built around them. The only disadvantage is that, unless the run is to be constructed against the house with a 'cat-flap' allowing free access, you have to take the cat in and out of the run! However, with a bit of Do-it-Yourself, you can successfully make your garden, in part or in its entirety, cat-safe, either using existing walls and fences that are *completely solid* with no holes, or by making up some new and secure fencing. Chicken wire should then be attached to the top of the fence, curving loosely inwards. Every time the cat reaches the wire and gets a grip, the wire will sag under its weight, forcing it to loosen its grip and fall back to the ground. It is important, however, to remember that cats are very good at digging underneath things, so the foundations of the wall or fence should be taken well down into the ground.

The 'flat' cat

Kittens will live very happily in flats, but certain factors must be taken into account. For a start, cats eat grass as a natural 'medicine' so a pot of grass should always be available to a cat denied outside access. This could be dug up from a friend's garden, but there are several different packs available at most pet shops, requiring only a few days to grow. If this all-important point is missed, then your house plants could be in for a severe pruning! Grass may cause the cat to vomit, but this is quite natural, and all part of the process. Of course, continual vomiting may have some other cause, and must be investigated by your vet.

If you are out at work all day, it is most unfair to leave a kitten confined and alone. Cats like company, and if that company cannot be provided by a human, then the kitten should have another feline friend to play with. Many breeders will refuse to sell a sole kitten if they know that it will be left alone for many hours, and may suggest that you should buy a pair together. Most breeders will offer you a discount on the price if you do this. If not, ask your vet if he knows of any nice, healthy and friendly 'moggie' kittens that need a good home.

Keep in contact with your kitten's breeder

Most breeders do not feel that their responsibility towards their kittens ends when the kitten is sold, and goes to its new home! Indeed, you will probably be asked to telephone after a few days to let him or her know how the kitten has settled down. If you have any problems or worries over your kitten, the breeder should be the one to tell. She will be more experienced with cats than you, and something that seems wrong to you may be perfectly normal and she will be able to reassure you that all is well. If you are thinking about showing or breeding your cat, again ask her advice: she will be able to help you fill in the necessary documentation, and will give you advice as to a suitable stud for breeding.

Even after many years, the breeder will be interested to hear any news of her 'progeny', and should always be informed if, for any reason, you have to part with your cat.

Chapter 4
Caring for your cat

When you buy your kitten, it should be in the peak of fitness and condition: and it is then your responsibility to keep it that way!

As well as having had the necessary inoculations, your kitten should also have been 'wormed' by the breeder before it left home. If not, consult your vet about a suitable course of treatment. It is not a good idea to buy a proprietary brand of worming treatment from a pet shop...much better to allow the vet to see the kitten and advise a suitable dosage.

In any event, your kitten should see the vet once a year for a thorough check-up, and also to have the necessary 'booster' inoculations.

Parasites

Parasites can cause severe distress to a cat, and you must monitor your cat for any signs of infestation. Ear mites will easily colonise in dirty ears, so inspect the ears frequently (about once a week), and keep them clean. The *outer* part of the ear can be simply cleaned with a cotton bud, dipped in either a cleansing lotion or a proprietary ear preparation. Signs of the presence of ear mites will include continual shaking of the head, and scratching at the ears. It is very easy to damage the delicate membranes in the ear, so if ear mites are suspected do not try to delve deep into the ear, but instead take the cat to your vet, who will be able to clear up the parasites with the correct medication.

Fleas are another form of parasite, and will be a great nuisance to all concerned. Although preferring the warm furry body of a cat, it is not unknown for them to hop off onto a human, for a quick 'bite' to eat! The symptoms of flea infestation are easy to recognize: the cat will scratch a lot, but the flea dirt can actually be seen, usually along the spine towards the back and under the chin. It looks rather like dark brown grit. In severe cases, you will actually be able to see the fleas hopping about. Again, it is not advisable to buy a preparation 'over the counter', but to see the vet: fleas and tape worms go hand-in-hand, so he will probably prescribe a worming dose as well. To prevent re-infestation, he will probably suggest that you use the flea powder or spray on a regular basis, especially if the cat is allowed to go outside where it is likely to meet other animals.

Tape worms are indeed carried by fleas, and will cause great discomfort to the unfortunate cat. They can be detected in many ways: in a young cat the abdomen will be distended, but will feel hard rather than soft: the cat may try to pull itself along the carpet or furniture with its front paws, as if trying to relieve an irritation in its anus; however, the most obvious sign is that of the last segments of the worm being excreted — they look like grains of rice adhering to the fur around the tail. The treatment is quick and easy, but the vet should be consulted in order that the correct preparation and dosage is administered. You will have to repeat the treatment several times to ensure that all of the worm has been expelled, and it is a good idea to 'worm' the cat on a regular basis about once every six months.

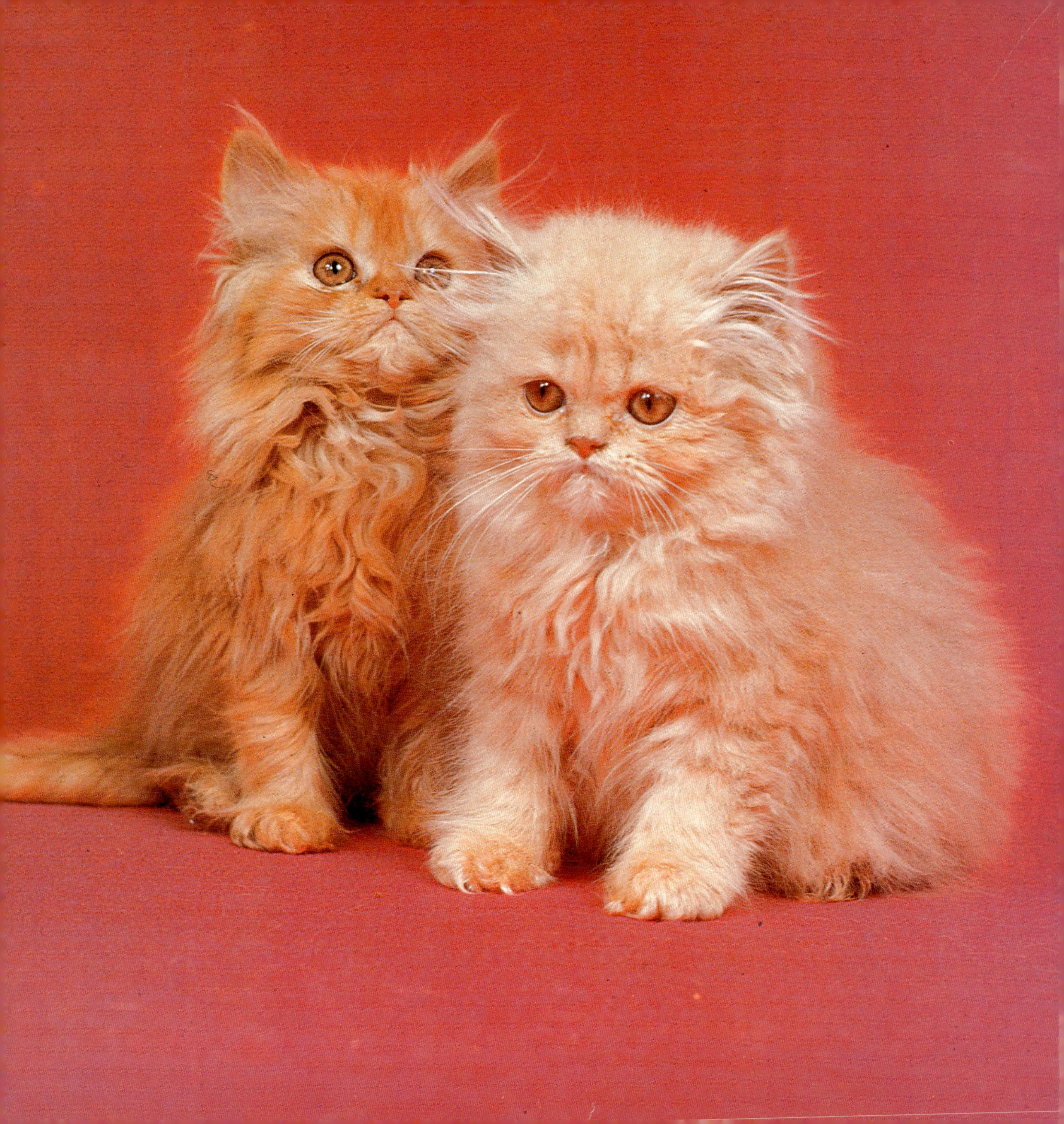

The parasites mentioned so far are the most common in cats: however there are several others that may infest the cat.

Ticks are usually associated with cattle and sheep, but may also grow on cats. They are often found in grass, and will attach themselves to the cat's head as it passes. Like fleas, they are blood-suckers, but actually bury their heads into the cat's skin whilst eating: when they are full they drop off, leaving a nasty weal behind. Ticks can be removed with tweezers, but you must be very careful to get the entire tick out, as if the head is left in it will cause infection. Usually it is better to allow the vet to remove them.

Mites will usually attack the head, ears and feet, and look like little orange specks. They can be treated with flea powder, or with a well-diluted disinfectant that is not toxic to cats. If in doubt, consult your vet.

Ringworm is one of the most unpleasant parasites, as it will infest not only animals but humans as well. It usually starts with a bald patch in the fur, which soon becomes scaley and sore. As there are other diseases, such as certain forms of eczema, that can look similar it is most important to take the cat to the vet for a correct diagnosis. Most forms of ringworm will 'fluoresce' when viewed in the dark under an ultra-violet 'Wood's Lamp', and the vet will soon be able to tell you if the cat has the very contagious ringworm, or something less drastic! In the event of a positive diagnosis of this condition, the cat must be isolated from all other animals and from children until the treatment has been completed and the condition cleared.

Infectious diseases

Generally speaking, the cat is a remarkably healthy creature. Properly fed, inoculated and free from parasites, there are few diseases that will befall it.

However, there are a few infectious diseases that, once contracted, must be dealt with promptly by your vet.

Feline Infectious Enteritis is gradually on the decline, as there are many brands of vaccine that will prevent the disease. This is the most important inoculation for any kitten, and no kitten should leave its mother until it has been done. Although this disease can be successfully treated in an adult cat, it is usually fatal in a kitten. The symptoms are a loss of appetite accompanied by diarrhoea, vomiting and dehydration. These first stages will be followed by a loss of coordination and the kitten will sit hunched up with a glassy stare. The kitten will be unable to follow any moving object, and if a pencil is waved slowly in front of its eyes, it will be unable to follow the movements, instead the head will jerk about as the kitten tries to cope. Correctly inoculated, however, there is little chance of any kitten contracting this disease.

Cat 'flu (Feline Rhinotracheitis) is a disease which attacks the upper respiratory tract. The first signs of this are runny eyes and nose, accompanied by coughing and sneezing. It is extremely contagious, and any cat showing these symptoms should be isolated immediately and the vet informed. It is most important to tell him that you think your cat may have the cat 'flu, as he may not want you to bring the infected cat into a busy surgery and suggest, instead, that you have a private appointment. He may even prefer to visit the cat at home. This illness is rarely fatal in an otherwise healthy cat, but can leave the cat with permanent runny eyes and catarrh. It is also possible for a cat that has been infected to become a 'carrier' of the disease for life: the vet will be able to make a test to see if this is the case.

There are several types of vaccine that will prevent the cat becoming infected, and your vet will be able to advise you on this.

Feline Infectious Peritonitis is a fairly uncommon disease in the cat, and usually occurs in younger animals. It is thought to be a viral infection, and the symptoms are swelling in the abdomen along with a lack of appetite. It is often fatal in younger cats.

Red and Cream Long-hair kittens

Watching 'Match of the Day' before bedtime

Feline Infectious Leukaemia is a viral infection that has been apparent for some years, but has only recently been recognized for what it is. There is no vaccine available at the time of writing. The best advice, and the most recent, will come from your vet — there is much unfounded gossip about this condition and the vet will reassure you if you have cause to worry. There is no evidence to suggest that humans can contract Feline Infectious Leukaemia.

Your cat's general health

As this is not intended to be a feline 'medical' book, it is impossible to mention all the ailments that a cat may possibly contract. With a careful eye, you will learn to detect when your cat is a little 'off colour'. Watch your new kitten carefully as it grows up; get to know how it reacts in various circumstances, what its usual eating and toilet habits are, how it normally walks, what its voice is like — the list could be endless. However, you will be able to notice if something is wrong very quickly, and be able to inform your vet of all the symptoms. It is a good idea to give your cat a 'check-over' once a week: check the whole body thoroughly, feeling for any unusual lumps and bumps, and watching for any signs of unusual swelling or lameness. A general sign that a cat is unwell is if the 'haws', or third eyelids are visible. Well before you have any reason to think that the cat is ill, make sure that you have registered with a local veterinary surgeon. Ask pet-owners in your area whom they would recommend, and if you bought your kitten from a local breeder, seek her advice as well.

Once you have found a vet whom you think you will be happy with, register your cat imme- if you have an emergency, he will know you and be able to offer you the help and advice you need.

Where to go for further information

North American Cat Associations

A.C.A. (American Cat Assiciation)
Secretary: Ms Susie Page, 10065 Foothill Bvd., Lake View Terrace, CA, U.S.A.

A.C.C. (American Cat Council)
Althea Frahm (President), P.O. Box 662, Pasadena, CA 91102

A.C.F.A. (American Cat Fanciers Association)
Ed Rugenstein, P.O. Box 203, Point Lookout, Missouri 67526

C.C.A. (Canadian Cat Association)
General Office, 14 Nelson Street West, Suite 5, Brampton, Ontario, Canada L6X 1B7

C.F.A. (Cat Fanciers Association)
Thomas H. Dent, Executive Manager, 1309 Allaire Ave, Ocean, N.J. 07712

C.C.F. (Cat Fanciers Federation)
Barbara Haley, Recorder, 9509 Montgomery Road, Cincinnati, Ohio 45242

C.C.F.F. (Crown Cat Fanciers Federation)
Sister Vincent, P.O. Box 34, Nazareth, Kentucky 40048

T.I.C.A. (The International Cat Association)
USA: Georgia Morgan (President), P.O. Box 2988, Harlingen, Tx 78551
UK: The Registrar, Orchard Cottage, Westcot Lane, Sparshot, Wantage, Oxon OX12 9PZ

U.C.F. (United Cat Federation)
Secretary: David Young, 6621 Thornwood Street, San Diego, CA 92111

Index

Numerals in **bold** type refer to the pages on which illustrations appear.

Abysinnian **32, 33**, 34
Angora 16

Balinese 22,**23**
Baskets 51
Bi-Colour Long-hair **12**
Birman 19, **22**
Black Long-hair 16
Blue Long-hair 16, **17**
Breeder 9, 10, 11, 14, 58
Breeding 13
British Short-hair 9, 24-31, 33, 39
    Black **26**, 26, **28**
    Blue **25**, 26, **27**
    Blue-Cream **6, 7, 29,** 28
    Cream **28**, 28
    Red Tabby **31**
    Silver Spotted **8**
    Silver Tabby 30, **30**
    Tabby 24, 30
    White **24**, 24
Brown Tabby Long-hair 16
Burmese **11, 14,** 26, 33, 39, 46-49, **56, 57**
    Blue 46,**48**
    Brown 39, 46, **48**
    Chocolate **44**, 46
    Cream 46
    Lilac 46, **56**
    Red 46, **47**
    Tortie 46

Cats 9, 63
Cat clubs 9, 13, 36, 45
Cat club 13, 61
Cat houses 58
Children with Cats 52, **53**
Chinchilla 15, **15**, 16, **16**
Colourpoint 19, **20** 21
Cornish Rex 33, 36-39, **38**
Cream Long-hair **60**

Dehydration 61
Devon Rex 33, 36-39, **36, 37, 38,** 54, 55
Diarrhoea 39, 61

Diet 54
Disinfectant 52

Ear mites 59
Eczema 61
Experimental breeds 22

Feeding *see* Nutrition
Feline Infectious Enteritis 13, 61
Feline Infectious Leukaemia 62
Feline Infectious Peritonitis 61
Feline Viral Rhinotracheitis 13, 61
Fleas 59, 61
Flu 13, 61
Foreign Short-hairs 9, 32-42
    Black 33, 42
    Blue 33, 42
    Lilac 33, 42
    White 33, **41**, 42

Governing Council of the Cat Fancy 9, 11, 22, 34, 36, 39, 42
Grooming **15**, **16**, 16, 22, 24, 39

Harness **57**,58
Havana 33, 39, **40**, 42
House training 52

Infectious diseases 61
Inoculations 9, 13

Judges 14, **14**

Kitten list 9
Korat 33, 39

Leukaemia 62
Litter trays 51, 52, **52**
Long-hair 9, 10, 15-23, 24, 33
    Bi-colour **12**
    Black 16
    Blue 16,**17**
    Brown Tabby 16
    Cream **60**
    Red **60**
    Tortoiseshell 16, **19**, 21
    White 16, **18**

Manx 30

Mites 61

Neutering 11, 13
Nutrition 24, 54-55

Oriental Spotted 39
Oriental Tabby 33, 39

Papers 11,
Parasites 59
Pedigree 11
Peritonitis 61
Persian 9, 10, 15-23
Pet shops 9, 58
Playing 11, 55

Queen 13

Red Long-hair **60**
Registration 11
Rex *see* Cornish and Devon Rex
Ringworm 61
Rumpy 30
Russian Blue 26, 33, 34-35, **34, 35**

Shows 9, 13, **14**, 14, 19, 45, 46
Siamese 10, 19, 22, 33, 42, **42, 43,** 42-45, 46
Spaying 13
Stumpy 30
Swimming cat 19

Tape worms 59
Teeth 11
Ticks 61
Toilet training 52, **52**
Tortoiseshell Long-hair 16, **19, 21**
Tortie-and-White Long-hair 16
Toys 55-56
Transfer 11
Turkish Van 19
Type 10, 13, 16, 33, 36, 39, 45

Vaccines 13, 61, 62
Veterinary surgeon 9, 61, 62
Vomiting 61

White Long-hair 16, 18
Worms 10, 59